Chinese Whispers

Chinoiserie in Britain 1650-1930

Edited by **David Beevers**

The Royal Pavilion & Museums, Brighton & Hove

Chinese Whispers

Chinoiserie in Britain 1650-1930

Published by The Royal Pavilion & Museums, Brighton & Hove, 2008
4-5 Pavilion Buildings, Brighton, East Sussex BN1 1EE, UK

on the occasion of the exhibition
Chinese Whispers: Chinoiserie in Britain 1650-1930
held at Brighton Museum & Art Gallery and the Royal Pavilion,
3 May – 2 November 2008

Supported by:
The Friends of the Royal Pavilion, Art Gallery & Museums, Brighton, Ian Askew, Elaine Evans, John Rank, Richard Sachs, Lady Judith Swire, the British Antique Dealers Association, and private individuals who wish to remain anonymous

Exhibition curated by David Beevers, Keeper of Fine Art, and organised by Nicola Coleby, Jody East and Helen Grundy, Exhibitions Section, Royal Pavilion & Museums, Brighton & Hove

The publication of the catalogue is supported by The Paul Mellon Centre for Studies in British Art, The Henry Moore Foundation, The Friends of the Royal Pavilion, Art Gallery & Museums, Brighton, and The Regency Society of Brighton & Hove

Editor: David Beevers

Catalogue picture research by Jody East
Designed by Nigel Cunningham and ingenious design
Printed in Great Britain by Cambridge University Press

ISBN 978-0-948723-71-1

Front cover illustration: B106 *Pair of monumental vases and covers*, Brian Haughton Gallery, London; **Endpapers:** C3 *Four sections of a Coromandel screen*, Leeds Museums & Galleries (Temple Newsam); **pp 2-3 illustration:** C5 *Cabinet on stand*, The Holburne Museum of Art, Bath (detail)

RENAISSANCE
SOUTH EAST
museums for
changing lives

The Henry Moore
Foundation

Contents

Sponsors of the Exhibition

Ian Askew Esq

British Antique Dealers' Association

Elaine Evans

The Friends of the Royal Pavilion, Art Gallery & Museums

John Rank Esq

Richard Sachs Esq

Lady Judith Swire

And those who wish to remain anonymous

Publication of the catalogue has been generously subsidised by The Paul Mellon Centre for Studies in British Art, The Henry Moore Foundation, The Friends of the Royal Pavilion, Art Gallery & Museums, Brighton and The Regency Society of Brighton & Hove

The Regency Society

The Henry Moore Foundation

C5 Cabinet on stand, The Holburne Museum of Art, Bath (detail)

Foreword

It is highly appropriate that the first major loan exhibition on the subject of chinoiserie for 70 years should be held in Brighton; for here, at the Royal Pavilion, is the greatest single expression of that fascination with the Orient which has haunted the imagination of the West for 400 years. Indeed, one of the aims of the exhibition is to provide a context for the dazzling interiors of the Royal Pavilion where, thanks to the generosity of Her Majesty the Queen, superb, deluxe chinoiserie objects collected or commissioned by King George IV specifically for his pleasure palace, will be displayed. The Beijing Olympics in 2008 has focussed attention on China and provides an added impetus to holding the exhibition at this time. The fascination of chinoiserie is the way in which one culture interprets and misunderstands another, yet succeeds in creating sumptuous and visually exciting works of art.

A25 *The Duke of Sussex's epergne*
Private collection

In preparing this exhibition we have been assisted by many other institutions and individuals. Without the supreme generosity of lenders and sponsors (both listed separately), the project could never have been fulfilled. We are indebted to those who have contributed their specialist knowledge both to the catalogue and more generally to the exhibition, notably to Mr James Lomax, Curator of Collections at Temple Newsam, Leeds, for his generosity in giving up so much time to assemble a quite outstanding array of chinoiserie silver and providing advice and contacts which have proved invaluable; to Dr Patrick Conner for his assistance in selecting pictures and prints, and for much help in other matters relating to his field of expertise; and to Dr Sarah Cheang for her witty and provocative interpretation of 20th century chinoiserie. Our gratitude is due also to the individual owners and curators of the lending institutions.

In addition, the exhibition curator, David Beevers, would like to thank particularly the following individuals:

Derek Adlam, Hélène Alexander, Ray Biggs, Mr and Mrs Anthony Du Boulay, Emile de Bruijn, Maureen Buja, Stephen Calloway, Richard Calvocoressi, Frances Collard, Sheila O'Connell, Howard Coutts, Paul Crane, Jon Culverhouse, Margaret Curson, Aileen Dawson, Oliver Fairclough, Helen Faulkner, John Finlay, Christopher Fish, Geoffrey Godden, Jessica Harrison-Hall, John Hardy, Christopher Hartop, Brian Haughton, Jonathan Horne, Professor Maurice Howard, Gareth Hughes, Helen Hughes, Lianne Jarrett, Stephen Jarrett, Professor Christiaan Jörg, Reino Liefkes, Loraine Long, Errol and Henriette Manners, Jonathan Marsden, Simon Martin, Sarah Medlam,

Geoffrey Munn, Tessa Murdoch, Lord Neidpath, Fred Nesta, Henry Potts, Andrew Renton, Noel Riley, Sir Hugh Roberts, John Sandon, Henry Smith, Timothy Stevens, Ian Stranack, Lisa White, Mr and Mrs Tom Walford, The Countess of Wemyss and March, Mr and Mrs Whitehead, Mr and Mrs Peter White, Stephen Wildman, Lady Willoughby de Eresby, Matthew Winterbottom, Christine Woods, Mr Hilary Young.

The dedication of a large number of staff, both past and present, and helpers at Brighton Museum & Art Gallery and the Royal Pavilion has enabled this exhibition to be realised. Special thanks are due to Mike Jones, former Head of Conservation & Design at Brighton Museum and the Royal Pavilion, whose formidable knowledge of, and insight into, the chinoiserie style has led to an exhibition design of real imagination. Gordon Grant, Senior Conservator at Brighton Museum and the Royal Pavilion, has worked tirelessly to ensure the success of this project.

The exhibition has been curated in-house by David Beevers, Keeper of Fine Art, with contributions from Stella Beddoe, Senior Keeper and Keeper of Decorative Art. It was organised by Exhibitions staff Nicola Coleby, Helen Grundy and Jody East, who have worked under great pressure to realise an extremely ambitious project.

Credit is also due to the following staff members and helpers:
All security staff at Brighton Museum and the Royal Pavilion, Robin Abbott, Sharon Bacon, Emma Booth, Diane Brandrett, Janet Brough, Camay Chapman-Cameron, Nigel Cunningham, Gaye Conley, Martin Ellis, Kevin Faithfull, Elaine Fayers, Lara Featherstone, Roy Flint, Mike Fox, Mary Goody, Su Hepburn, Ray Martin, Lucy Mutter, Suzie Plumb, Sarah Posey, Don Sale, Hannah Schafer, Abigail Thomas, Eleanor Thompson, Russell Webb, Heather Wood, Karen Wraith, Paula Wrightson.

Finally, I would like to thank China Now and all those individuals who have expressed enthusiasm for the project and helped in numerous ways throughout its development.

Janita Bagshawe, Director of the Royal Pavilion
Head of Museums, Brighton & Hove.

List of Lenders

Her Majesty the Queen

Amgueddfa Cymru, National Museum of Wales

Ashmolean Museum, Oxford

Birmingham Museums & Art Gallery

The Bowes Museum, Barnard Castle, Co. Durham

The Trustees of the British Museum

The Burghley House Collection

Burton Constable Foundation

Stephen Calloway

The Chippendale Society

Mr and Mrs Stephen Clark

Patrick Conner

English Heritage (The Heaven Closet, Little Castle, Bolsover Castle, Derbyshire)

Erddig, The Yorke Collection (The National Trust)

Evan Bedford Library of Furniture History

The Fan Museum, London

Christopher Fish, Guernsey

The Rosalinde and Arthur Gilbert Collection on loan to the Victoria and Albert Museum

The Worshipful Company of Goldsmiths

Grimsthorpe and Drummond Castle Trust

John Hardy

Brian Haughton Gallery, London

The Holburne Museum of Art, Bath

Jonathan Horne

Jonathan Horne Antiques Ltd, London

Leeds Museums & Galleries

National Gallery, London

Trustees of the National Museums Scotland

Pallant House Gallery, Chichester

RIBA Library, Drawings and Archives Collections

Sampson & Horne Antiques, London

Salisbury & South Wiltshire Museum

Trustees of the Armouries

The Royal Pavilion & Museums, Brighton & Hove

Victoria & Albert Museum

Tom Walford

Wartski, London

The Earl of Wemyss and March, K.T

John Whitehead Collection

The Whitworth Art Gallery, University of Manchester

Lady Willoughby de Eresby

Witney Antiques

Worcester Porcelain Museum

and all those who wish to remain anonymous

'Mand'rin only is the man of taste'[1]
17th and 18th Century Chinoiserie in Britain

Chinoiserie as a term used to describe a European fantasy vision of China and the east (including India, Persia and Japan) is an expression of relatively recent invention. It first appeared in dictionaries in 1883 when it meant Chinese conduct or, oddly, a 'notion' of China. The *Oxford English Dictionary* (1971 edition) repeats this but includes Chinese art in the definition. Chinoiserie in the sense art historians use it today may have made an early appearance in France in 1911 in J Guérin's *La Chinoiserie en Europe au XVIIIe Siècle* but it was not commonly used until after 1945. What is certain is that the word was unknown in the 17th and 18th centuries. 'Chinois', however, the French for Chinese, appeared as early as 1625 in Samuel Purchas's *Purchas his Pilgrimes*; thereafter it occurs quite frequently to mean 'the Chinese'.

At this period, European interpretations and imitations of Chinese and East Asian artefacts were known as 'Japan work', 'India work', or 'China work'. An inventory of 1614 drawn up for the Earl of Northampton refers both to an imported 'China guilt (sic) cabinet' and English articles, for instance a 'China worke table and frame' and a 'field bedstead of China worke'. These almost certainly refer to European interpretations of Chinese and Japanese lacquer[2]. In 1615 Thomas Howard, Earl of Arundel, asked his wife to buy a quilt for 'ye bedde of Jappan'. This must have been European and is an early instance of the geographical vagueness associated with everything connected with 'the Indies', a term that encompassed much of Asia and the Americas.

Early Accounts of China

For Europe and for Britain China was the mystical land of Cathay, the name given in England in the Middle Ages to the 4000 year old civilization which lay beyond the confines of what was then known. The Venetian Marco Polo (1254-1324) may or may not have lived for seventeen years in China, but his reputed travels in Asia between1271 and 1295 provided the foundation on which many subsequent accounts were based. The *Description of the World*, based on Polo's account and published in 1298, became an epitome of an alternative reality, remote from anything known in Europe. In the propagation of the myth of Cathay Polo was soon joined by the entirely fictitious *Travels of Sir John Mandeville*, compiled anonymously in the mid 14th century. Mandeville, whose very name is an invention, provided an account which further stimulated belief in China as a land of wonder. A compound of all the most far-fetched stories from Greek writers together

Fig1.1 A detail of the chinoiserie panelling in the Heaven Room at Bolsover Castle, Derbyshire, c.1616-1619. English Heritage

with genuine travel accounts, this fairy-tale evocation of Africa, Egypt and the Orient was translated throughout Europe before 1500.

Published references to China naturally stimulated an interest in the products of the country. Small quantities of Chinese artefacts had entered Europe by the silk route through central Asia since antiquity, but it was not until after the Portuguese explorer Vasco da Gama's discovery of the sea route to the west coast of India via the Cape of Good Hope in 1498 that maritime contact between Europe and Asia was established. Henceforth, Chinese products, notably silk and porcelain, found their way to Europe in some quantity. By the early 17th century, the Dutch and English East India Companies were supplying the market for luxury goods from Asia. The first four voyages of the English East India Company, between 1601 and 1607, were to Bantam in Java where quantities of porcelain were acquired as 'private trade' by the ship's crew.

Because Chinese porcelain was so unlike anything produced in Europe, it was regarded as a rare substance imbued with magical qualities. It could represent both newness and an ancient civilization. William Cecil, Lord Burghley (1520-1598) mounted his Chinese porcelain in silver (see cat nos B41-B44) as did Lettice, Countess of Leicester, whose possessions in 1634 included a 'pursland boule' (porcelain bowl) with 'guilt foote and guilt cover'. Silver settings adapted exotic objects to European taste whilst also masking cracks and blemishes; they also drew attention to the importance and rarity of the object. These early porcelains were often displayed in cabinets of curiosity or 'Wunderkammern' (see also p. 39).

Masques and the Theatre

The fascination with China and its wares inspired an elaborate masque by Ben Jonson entitled *'The Key Keeper: An Entertainment at Britain's Burse'* (1609), which was performed before King James 1st at the opening of the New Exchange in the Strand, London. The Keeper invites the royal party to meet a shopkeeper, a 'China man' who draws attention to the magical qualities of porcelain and proclaims that 'there's not a trifle in this whole shop that is not mysterious'. The theme was taken up in Jonson's play *Epicoene, or the Silent Woman*, (1609-10), which satirises female extravagance in the character of Mrs Otter, 'the rich china woman, that the courtiers visited so often', and makes an early link between transgressive women, madness and things Chinese: 'go with me to Bedlam, to the china-houses and to the Exchange'. The voyeuristic and effeminate Sir Amorous La-Foole spies on the ladies going into the china-houses and there is a clear suggestion that these shops were places where illicit love affairs took place, a theme taken up later in the century by William Wycherley in *The Country Wife* (1675).[3] Jonson is clearly fascinated by China; his source of information was Juan Gonzalez de Mendoza's *Historie of the Great and Mightie Kingdome of China, and the Situation Thereof*, 1585 (English translation 1588), and

Fig1.2 Ivory ground japanned cabinet-on-stand with silvered stand and cresting, c.1695-1700. The Holburne Museum of Art, Bath

The Key Keeper includes a hymn of praise: 'Oh your Chinese! The only wise nation under the Sun: they had the knowledge of all manner of arts and letters, many thousand years before any of these parts could speak. Sir John Mandeville was the first that brought science from thence...'.[4] Jonson treated China both as a land of fantasy and as a source of ancient wisdom, a stock theme which emerges again and again in this period.

The Earliest Chinoiseries

Imported Chinese commodities led to European imitations and interpretations. An early surviving attempt to emulate oriental lacquer is the ballot box dated 1619 used by the East India Company and now owned by the Saddlers' Company. A consignment of oriental lacquer had arrived in London in 1614 and the Saddlers' Company box may have been made in imitation.[5] Another very rare survival from this period is the set of four low stools dating from c.1635-40 in the Long Gallery at Ham House, their bulbous turned legs japanned black and decorated with chinoiseries. At Bolsover Castle, Derbyshire, the panelling in the Heaven Room of the Little Castle is painted with gilt chinoiseries.[6] This room, originally a bedroom closet, is the earliest surviving chinoiserie interior in Britain, dating from c.1616-1619. Probably the work of a Netherlandish artist, the motifs consist of orientalised pastoral scenes (fig 1.1, cat C1).[7] These rare early manifestations of chinoiserie are extremely interesting, but it was not until the late 17th century that there was a surge of interest in the style. This is because there was a sharp growth in imports from China and Japan, including lacquer and porcelain, which, because of high prices, caused an imbalance of trade and thus stimulated a demand which could not be matched by the supply. The expense of Japanese and Chinese lacquer meant that it remained an élite taste.

Lacquer and 'Japan'

In the 17th and early 18th centuries, incised and polychrome Chinese lacquer was known as 'bantam ware' in England after the Dutch port on the west coast of Java from which much of it was shipped. The English East India Company established their first factory (a combination of a fort and a warehouse) at Bantam in the early 17th century. In the following century this distinctive lacquer was imported via India's south east Coromandel coast and thus became known as coromandel ware. In England it was sometimes called 'cutt-work', 'burnt Japan' or 'India work' and was used to panel rooms or was cut up to form cabinets. A famous entry in John Evelyn's diary exemplifies the geographical confusion of the time. Evelyn records a visit on 30 July 1683 to a neighbour, Mr Bohun, 'whose whole house is a cabinet of all elegancies, especially Indian; in the hall are contrivances of Japan screens ... the landscape of the screens represents the manner of living and country of the Chinese'. At Chatsworth in 1683 the Duchess's closet was panelled in

Fig1.3 Illustration from Stalker and Parker's *Treatise of Japaning and Varnishing*, 1688

'hollow burnt Japan', and examples survive today at Burton Agnes, Yorkshire, and Drayton, Northamptonshire, where the Duchess of Norfolk's closet has coromandel lacquer panels. The room was intended to house oriental porcelain.[8] Lacquer or japanned cabinets, sometimes used to house rarities and curiosities, were frequently found in bedchambers or closets occupied by women. After the bed, such cabinets were the most expensive items of furniture in the bedroom (fig1.2, cat C5).

Imitation and genuine lacquer was known as 'japan' because of the confusion of countries of the East and because much lacquer did come from Japan via the Dutch East India Company. The imitation of Asian lacquer was facilitated by the publication in 1688 of John Stalker and George Parker's *Treatise of Japaning and Varnishing*, which went through four editions in a year. The title page announces more than 100 patterns 'for Japan-work in imitation of the Indians', for tables, picture frames, cabinets and boxes. Significantly, much of the furniture related to the bedroom and the dressing room, rooms in which chinoiserie was particularly favoured, and the work was dedicated to the Countess of Derby, a skilled japanner, as japanning was seen as a particularly female accomplishment (see cat E2, E3). Lacquered surfaces complemented the mysterious translucence of porcelain and provided surface textures thought particularly to appeal to women. One of the designs, bizarrely intended for a lady's comb box, is a scene of Chinese torture derived from an engraving on page 171 of the English translation (1669, second edition 1673) of Johan Nieuhof's *An Embassy from the East India Company of the United Provinces to the Grand Tartar Cham Emperor of China*. Nieuhof, steward to the ambassador of the Dutch embassy to China in 1655, clearly regarded torture as forming part of the image of the East.[9] His book was a major source of chinoiserie motifs throughout Europe in the 17th and 18th centuries. The English edition had over 100 engravings of Chinese scenes copied from the original plates by several printmakers including Wenceslaus Hollar and Francis Place (cat E1).

Stalker and Parker's designs were hybrid, sensual and exotic; japanning was even likened to make-up: 'as painting has made an honourable provision for our bodies, so japanning [preserves] our furniture'. Motifs from the East could of course be 'helped' in their proportions 'where they are lame and defective, and make them more pleasant, yet altogether Antick' (ie bizarre or grotesque). Images were taken from Chinese export porcelain, lacquer screens and, as we have seen, prints found in Johan Nieuhof's *Embassy*. Stalker and Parker's work could be used to create an orient in miniature; the engravings seemed to embody whim and novelty and to abide by no rules known to Europe.

'Sharawadgi'

In 1685 Sir William Temple, who had been ambassador to the Hague in 1668, attempted to analyse the nature of Chinese gardening, but his observations, published as an essay entitled 'Upon the Gardens of Epicurus' in *Miscellanea* (1690), had a wider application, he thought, to Chinese art in general: 'But their greatest reach of imagination is employed in contriving figures, where the beauty shall be great, and strike the eye, but without any order or disposition of parts ... and though we have hardly any notion of this sort of beauty, yet they have a particular word ... they say the sharawadgi is fine ... And whoever observes the work upon the best India gowns, or the painting upon their best screens or purcellans, will find their beauty is all of this kind [that is] without order'. Temple had read Nieuhof, Marco Polo and Athanasius Kircher's *China Monumentis qua Sacris Profanis ... Illustrata* (Amsterdam, 1667) and he hugely admired the Chinese sage Confucius, about whom he wrote in his essay *Of Heroic Virtue* (1690). 'Sharawadgi' was not in fact a Chinese term at all but derived from a Japanese word connoting asymmetry.[10]

This 'beauty without any order' even entered aspects of the Baroque theatre. Elkanah Settle's *The Fairy Queen* (1692), with music by Purcell and a libretto based on Shakespeare's *A Midsummer Night's Dream*, had, according to the stage directions, dancing monkeys, Chinese lovers, 'china-work' pedestals rising from the stage and 'The Architecture, the Trees, the Plants, the Fruit, the Birds ... quite different from what we have in this part of the World'.[11]

A Reaction to Classicism

An interior containing oriental export wares and European imitations and interpretations offered contemporaries an escape from classicism into a world of sophisticated baroque illusion, similar in some respects to the theatre. It was precisely this reaction to classicism which inspired the dismay of commentators who sensed a retreat from reason and taste and a descent into a morally ambiguous world based on hedonism, sensation and values perceived to be feminine. The 3rd Earl of Shaftesbury (1671-1713) saw chinoiserie and the fashion for Chinese objects as frivolous and opposed to the paradigms of art derived from Greece and Rome. Yet he was half seduced himself: 'Effeminacy pleases me. The Indian figures, the Japan work, the enamel strikes my eye. The luscious colours and glossy paint gain upon my fancy ... But what ensues? ... How is it possible I should then come to taste the beauties of an Italian master, or of a hand happily formed on nature and the ancients'.[12] This disjunction between critics and intellectuals and the taste for chinoiserie continued well into the 19th century.

The Rococo and Chinoiserie

In the 1750s the fashion reached the height of its popularity in Britain. The author and architect Robert Morris (c.1702-1754) was one of many who complained that the Chinese taste consisted of 'mere whims and chimera, without rules or order, it requires no fertility of genius to put in execution. The principles are a good choice of chains and bells and different colours of paints. As to the serpents, dragons, monkeys, &c. they, like the rest of the beauties, may be cut in paper and pasted anywhere.' He complained of oriental 'trifles … esteemed when it is the fashion to be ridiculous'.[13] It is worth asking why, when chinoiserie was disreputable according to classical canons of taste, it should have been so widespread. It can be no coincidence that the taste was particularly associated with the French-inspired rococo style, for this too was anti-classical and linked with a relaxation from rules and antiquity. Both styles relied on irregularity, fantasy and asymmetry. Hogarth in the *Analysis of Beauty* (1753) argued that straight lines were unnatural and serpentine lines which led 'the eye a wanton kind of chase' were truly beautiful. Hogarth was unsympathetic to chinoiserie and he particularly disliked the 'paltry' imitation of Chinese buildings, but his advocacy of novelty, variety and surprise accorded with an aesthetic which could embrace rococo, gothic, and chinoiserie. The near mass production of engravings after François Boucher, Jacques de Lajoue and Jean Pillement spread the chinoiserie style of Watteau and Boucher throughout Europe. John Ingram's engravings after Boucher, published in England in the 1740s, were particularly important in furthering the taste. Boucher's chinoiseries can be traced to printed sources such as Arnoldus Montanus's *Gedenkwaerdige Gesantschappen der Oost-Indische Maatschappy (Memorable Missions of the East India Company)*, published in Amsterdam in 1669. Montanus had intended to portray Japan not China, thus adding to the confusion.[14] The use of motifs from these sources by designers meant that much chinoiserie produced in this country was inspired by Chinese themes inflected through French eyes.

Exotic dress fitted the rococo, a style which was colourful, frivolous and elegant. It is significant that Father Jean Attiret's description of the gardens at Yuanmingyuan, near Beijing, first published in 1749 in France and translated into English in 1752 as *A Particular Account of the Emperor of China's Gardens near Pekin*, spoke of 'beautiful disorder' and a 'wandering as far as possible from all the Rules of Art'. Attiret's *Account*, which went into three further editions in the 1760s, provided further justification for an association of asymmetry with chinoiserie. It is no coincidence that the works of Sir William Temple were reprinted in 1757, at the height of the Chinese mania, for Temple's well-known concept of 'sharawadgi', or asymmetry, was, like Attiret's 'beautiful disorder', in harmony with the rococo fashion. Horace Walpole wrote in 1750: 'I am almost as fond of the Sharawaggi, or Chinese want of symmetry in buildings, as in grounds or gardens'.[15] Walpole later dissociated himself from chinoiserie, but in the early 1750s this most famous proponent of gothic saw in both the gothic and Chinese styles 'a whimsical air of novelty that is very pleasing'. Remote respectively in time and place, gothic and Chinese when used together in a spirit of architectural experimentation could make old motifs new and fresh. Above all, both styles were profoundly anti-classical. A rash of pattern books published in the 1750s conflated the two fashions so that Chinese and gothic became almost interchangeable. The favoured gothic motif of the ogee arch with its curving

Fig1.4 Chinese furniture from Thomas Chippendale's *Gentleman and Cabinet Maker's Director*, 1754

lines shared the sinuous quality of much Chinese decoration. In 1752 William and John Halfpenny's *Chinese and Gothic Architecture Properly Ornamented* had plates in which pagoda roofs intermingle with turrets and battlements and, most famously, Thomas Chippendale's *Gentleman and Cabinet Maker's Director* (1754) included fantastically elaborate engravings of furniture in the Chinese and gothic tastes (fig 1.4).

Other factors that inspired the mid century explosion of chinoiserie may be briefly considered. In 1735 Jean-Baptiste Du Halde published in Paris his *Description...de l'empire de la Chine*. This was translated into English by John Watts in 1736 as *A Description of the Empire of China and Chinese Tartary, together with the Kingdom of Korea and Tibet*. Du Halde's book was a compendium of unpublished French Jesuit accounts of China in which the country is praised for its stability and its ethical system based on Confucius. So popular was the work that another translation by Edward Cave was published in 1738 and 1741. As an undergraduate at Cambridge, Walpole read the first French edition and was full of enthusiasm.[16] Du Halde became the standard source of information on China throughout the 18th century. Although undoubtedly influential in promoting a climate of opinion favourable to the country, the plates were poor and borrowed motifs from Nieuhof's *Embassy*, making them even less Chinese.

In 1755 David Garrick staged *The Chinese Festival*, based on a French ballet, *Les Fêtes Chinoises*. It was a disastrous failure, despite the lavish sets and costumes, due to anti-French sentiment (Britain was about to go to war with France). The sets may have been re-used in Arthur Murphy's *The Orphan of China* (1759), an adaptation of a genuine Chinese play published in Du Halde's *Description*. Also in 1755 a pantomime, *Proteus, or Harlequin in China*, was produced at Drury Lane.[17] All these mid-century productions inflamed the Chinese mania, as did the taste for tea, rapidly becoming the national drink.

The China Drink

Tea consumption was so widespread that annual East India Company imports increased from 214,000 pounds in 1713 to 32 million pounds in 1813.[18] Much of this increase was due to William Pitt's Commutation Act of 1784, which replaced the high import duties on tea, often amounting to 100 per cent, by a flat 12½ per cent of the value of tea imported. Tea drinking was a fundamental part of polite society; much of the interest in both Chinese export wares and chinoiserie arose from the desire to create appropriate settings for the ritual of tea drinking. The service of tea was seen as an essentially feminine activity and artefacts of Chinese inspiration or origin were associated by some commentators with gossiping women. Jonathan Swift in his *Journal of a Modern Lady* (1728) wrote 'Let me now survey / our madam o'er her evening tea'. The company is described as 'All mad to speak and none to hearken / They set the very lapdog barking / Their chattering

makes a louder din / Than fishwives o'er a cup of gin'. Jonas Hanway's *An Essay on Tea* (1756) provocatively linked tea to laziness, gossip in women, and effeminacy in men.[19] The acme of the association of China, women and tea is the Chinese Room at Claydon House, Buckinghamshire, created by Luke Lightfoot, a carver of genius, in the 1760s (fig1.5). Here the pagoda-like tea alcove is carved with an extraordinary array of rococo chinoiserie detail probably derived from motifs in Matthew (or Matthias) Darly and George Edwards's *A New Book of Chinese Designs Calculated to Improve the Present Taste* (1754). The form of the alcove may be traced to plate LXV of Ince and Mayhew's *Universal System of Household Furniture* (1762). Here was the perfect setting for tea to be served to the Countess Verney and her guests; appropriately enough, the carvings include Chinese figures taking tea.

The 1740s were a particularly vigorous period of trade between China and Britain and resulted in an increase in goods imported. In 1747, 14 ships sailed between London and Canton, a number not equalled until 1764.[20] Wares from China inspired emulation and added to the effusion of chinoiserie in the 1750s and 1760s, though it seems clear that people in the 18th and early 19th centuries were not as concerned as we are with the distinction between Chinese objects and Western interpretations of them. Lady Temple's dressing room at Stowe, for instance, contained Indian printed cotton hangings, a 'Japan' cabinet and a view of Peking (Beijing); but these could have been supplemented by chinoiserie furniture and silver. Lightness and elegance were what mattered.[21] Where apartments were decorated with Chinese export wallpapers appropriate furnishings were required. Chippendale's lattice-pattern chair backs have their origin in motifs from Chinese bridges depicted on porcelain and wallpaper.

Women and Chinoiserie

It has been noted how chinoiserie and oriental artefacts were closely connected with notions of femininity and female patronage. We have seen how japanning, the imitation of oriental lacquer, was considered to be a particularly female accomplishment. The designs of Pillement and others, published in *The Ladies Amusement; or, whole art of Japanning Made Easy* (two eds, c1758 and 1762) make the association clear. As late as 1828 Mrs Arbuthnot, a close friend of the Duke of Wellington, described 'a japan cabinet I painted last year … The cabinet is really excessively pretty'.[22] The taste for Chinese export lacquer screens was one associated with 'fair connoisseurs' by John Gilbert Cooper in his *Letters Concerning Taste* (1771), which rehearses a whole series of stock criticisms: 'what shall we say of the taste and judgement of those who [collect] pieces where neither perspective, nor proportion, nor conformity to nature are observed … no genuine beauty is to be found in whimsical and grotesque figures, the monstrous offspring of wild imagination, undirected by nature and truth'.[23] Chippendale, in the third edition of his *Director* (1762), warned of the

Fig1.5 The Chinese Room at Claydon House, Buckinghamshire. The National Trust

Fig1.6 Chair by William and John Linnell from the Chinese Bedroom at Badminton House, c.1754. Victoria & Albert Museum

weakness of Chinese fret-back chairs and suggested that such chairs would be 'very proper for a lady's Dressing Room; especially if it is hung with India [ie Chinese] paper'.

Women's bedrooms, dressing rooms and, later, drawing rooms were frequently hung with expensive hand-painted Chinese wallpaper and furnished with oriental porcelain and, occasionally, chinoiserie furniture. Bedrooms, as we have seen, were favoured spaces for Chinese experiments and the fantastic birds and figures on Chinese export wallpaper seemed particularly appropriate to the land of dreams. These light, informal, feminine spaces formed a marked contrast with the more traditionally masculine rooms. At Wanstead in 1724 Lady Castlemaine's apartment consisted of a parlour hung with 'China paper' and an antechamber, bedroom, dressing room and closet all furnished with 'China silk'.[24] The Chinese Bedroom at Badminton, Gloucestershire, was hung with a Chinese paper and supplied by William and John Linnell in about 1754 with what amounts to the first bedroom suite, all in a fantastic chinoiserie style. It is most likely that it was the Duchess of Beaufort, rather than the 4th Duke, who was responsible for selecting the Chinese style (fig 1.6, cat C8).[25] At Carton, County Kildare, Lady Kildare created in about 1759 the 'India Paper Drawing Room', probably the earliest surviving drawing room in the Chinese taste. Against a blue background, she attached cut-out fancifully shaped panels of Chinese wallpaper.[26] The drawing room at Dalemain, Cumbria, has a surviving Chinese wallpaper hung in about 1760. A later example of female agency survives at Temple Newsam, Leeds, where, in 1827, Lady Hertford, intimate companion of King George IV, installed a Chinese paper in the former Best Dining Room, which then became her new Blue Drawing Room (fig 1.7). In 1806 the paper had been given by George, when Prince Regent, to Lady Hertford's mother, Frances, Lady Irwin. Lady Hertford further embellished the paper with lively figures and birds cut from John James Audubon's *The Birds of America*.[27] It is significant that the dining room, regarded as masculine space, was transformed into a drawing room, seen as women's territory, by the installation of Chinese wallpaper. Dining rooms were rarely decorated in the Chinese style, although Chippendale provided designs for sideboard tables with frets and pierced decoration in the Chinese manner (*Gentleman and Cabinet-Maker's Director,* 1754 edition, plates XXXV to XL; retained in the 1762 edition plates LVI to LXI). The taste for chinoiserie continued into the 1770s, adding an exotic element to otherwise neo-classical interiors at, for instance, Harewood House and Nostell Priory, both in Yorkshire.

Chinoiserie interiors usually contained Chinese export porcelain vases and figures. Writers continued to associate the acquisition of porcelain with rapacious and irrational women, even going so far as to suggest mental instability. In 1753 Joseph Warton wrote of an imaginary visit to Bedlam with Dean Swift. He describes the insane Lady Brittle, driven mad by the loss

Fig 1.7 The Chinese Drawing Room at Temple Newsam House, Leeds. Leeds Museums & Galleries

of a China mandarin and unable to distinguish Chelsea porcelain from 'true Nankin'.[28] John Gay wrote in 1725 'China's the passion of her soul; / A cup, a plate, a dish, a bowl / can kindle wishes in her breast, / inflame her joy, or break her rest'. The point is well made in Hogarth's *Marriage à la Mode: The Tête à Tête* (c.1743). Here the artist uses an array of grinning Budai figures (parodies of the Chinese god of happiness) on the mantelpiece, a chinoiserie clock-girandole, and a fire screen with a Chinese fabric to suggest a link between the Chinese taste and dissipation. The wife's suggestive glance and coquettish stretch imply that she has taken a lover, to whom she may be signalling with her mirror. Her husband has been whoring; the dog retrieves a woman's bonnet from his pocket. The scene evokes the last four lines of James Cawthorn's poem *Of Taste, An Essay* (1756): 'On ev'ry shelf a Joss divinely stares, / Nymphs laid on chintzes sprawl upon our chairs; / While o'er our cabinets Confucius nods, / Midst porcelain elephants and China gods' (fig 1.8, cat F6). And this association continued into the nineteenth century. Charles Lamb, in his essay 'Old China' in *The Last Essays of Elia* (1833), admitted: 'I have an almost feminine partiality for old china'. The corollary of this was that only effeminate men showed an interest in porcelain and things Chinese. The *Connoisseur* described in 1755 a 'male beauty' who repairs his 'battered countenance' in a dressing room adorned

Fig1.8 William Hogarth, Marriage à *la Mode: The Tète à Tète*, c.1743. National Gallery, London

with 'little images of Pagods.'[29] The same publication suggested a chinoiserie interior in a gentleman's room revealed a corrupted taste and was fit only for men 'of delicate make and silky constitution'.[30]

Satirised and criticised, associated with female sensibility and rapacity, chinoiserie allowed a welcome injection of the exotic into the classical mainstream. The number of surviving Chinese rooms in country houses testifies to its appeal in providing a sensual aesthetic based on irregularity, fantasy, and otherness.

David Beevers

1 The quotation is from James Cawthorn's satirical poem 'Of Taste: An Essay' (written c.1761, published 1771) quoted in William W Appleton, *A Cycle of Cathay: The Chinese Vogue in England during the Seventeenth and Eighteenth Centuries*, New York: Columbia University Press, 1951, p.90

2 Helena Hayward, 'The Chinese influence on English Furniture' in *The Westward influence of the Chinese Arts, Colloquies on Art and Archaeology in Asia*, 3, Percival David Foundation, 1972, p.57

3 Linda Levy Peck, *Consuming Splendor: Society and Culture in Seventeenth-Century England*, Cambridge University Press, 2005, p.65

4 James Knowles, 'Cecil's shopping centre', *Times Literary Supplement*, February 7, 1997, pp 14-15

5 Ralph Edwards, 'The Master of the Saddler's Ballot Box', *Burlington Magazine*, no 68, May, 1936 pp 232-235

6 Peter Thornton and Maurice Tomlin, 'The Furnishing and Decorating of Ham House', *Furniture History*, vol XVI, 1980, pp 26-27

7 Lucy Worsley, Bolsover Castle, (guide book), English Heritage, 2000, p.24. I am indebted to Helen Hughes of English Heritage for confirming the remarkably early date of this interior

8 Tessa Murdoch, 'Les cabinets de porcelaines', in *Pagodes et Dragons: Exotisme et fantaisie dans l'Europe rococo 1720-1770*, exh cat, Musée Cernuschi, Paris, 2007, p.46

9 Philippa Tristram, 'Sprawling dragons, squatting pagods, and clumsy mandarines', *Georgian Group Journal*, 1995, p.3 and Leslie B Grigsby, 'Johan Nieuhoff's *Embassy*: An inspiration for relief decoration on English stoneware and earthenware', *The Magazine Antiques*, January 1993, p.173

10 Ciaran Murray, 'Sharawadgi Resolved', *Garden History*, Winter 1998, p.208

11 William W Appleton, *A Cycle of Cathay*, op.cit., p.71

12 David Porter, *Ideographia: The Chinese Cipher in Early Modern Europe California*: Stanford University Press, 2001, p.166. The quotation is from *Shaftesbury's Soliloquy, or, Advice to an Author* (1710), republished in *Characteristicks of Men, Manners, Opinions, Times* (1711)

13 Robert Morris, *Architectural Remembrancer*, 1751, quoted in Eileen Harris, *British Architectural Books and Writers*, Cambridge: Cambridge University Press, 1990, p.220

14 Perrin Stein, 'Boucher's chinoiseries: some new sources', *Burlington Magazine*, vol CXXXVIII, No 1122, September 1996, pp 598-604

15 David Porter, 'From Chinese to Goth: Walpole and the Gothic Repudiation of Chinoiserie', *Eighteenth-Century Life*, vol 23, 1999, p.50

16 Ibid, p.50

17 Hugh Honour, *Chinoiserie*, London: John Murray, 1961 (1973 ed.), p.126

18 Anthony Farrington, *Trading Places: The East India Company and Asia 1600-1834*, London: The British Library, 2002, p.94

19 David Porter, *Ideographia*, op.cit., p.194

20 Email from Patrick Conner 10/7/2007 quoting Hosea B Morse, *Chronicles of the East India Company Trading to China*, V, p.198-202. I am grateful to Patrick Conner and Emile de Bruijn for helping me elucidate why chinoiserie reached its apogee in Britain in the1750s.

21 John Cornforth, *Early Georgian Interiors*, New Haven and London: Yale University Press, 2004, p.264

22 Hugh Honour, *Chinoiserie*, op.cit., p.126

23 William W Appleton, *A Cycle of Cathay*, op.cit., p.107

24 John Cornforth, *Early Georgian Interiors*, op.cit., p.257

25 Christopher Wilk, (ed.), *Western Furniture 1350 to the Present Day*, London: Philip Wilson, 1996, p.104

26 Dana Arnold, *The Georgian Country House: Architecture, Landscape and Society*, Gloucester: Sutton Publishing, 2003, p.92

27 Anthony Wells-Cole, *Historic paper Hangings from Temple Newsam and other English Houses*, Leeds City Art Galleries, 1983, pp 14-15 and Robert McCracken Peck, 'Cutting up Audubon for science and art', *The Magazine Antiques*, vol CLXIV, no 4, October 2003, pp 104-113

28 William W Appleton, *A Cycle of Cathay*, op.cit., p.108

29 David Porter, *Ideographia*, op. cit., p.189 and note 1

30 Patrick Conner, *Oriental Architecture in the West*, London: Thames & Hudson, 1979, p.59

'Prodigious Charming Pots...'[1] British Chinoiserie Ceramics

Chinese porcelain comes to Europe

Porcelain has been made in China since the late 6th century AD. It was soon exported throughout Asia and even as far as Egypt but failed to reach Europe until the mid 14th century.[2] After that pieces made isolated appearances, probably by way of Venetian trade links with the Middle East and the silk route across central Asia and occasionally by sea, during a period when China was isolated from world trade. Marco Polo was among the first Europeans to name porcelain, when he compared its white surface with cowry shells, known as *porceletta in Italian*, although he was probably following a usage (and a confusion) already current.[3] He remarks that bowls the colour of azure could be obtained very cheaply in Qingbai and that

'...In that province is a city, named Ti-min-gui [Jingdedzhen], where they make the most beautiful cups in the world; they are of porcelain...'[4]

Such items were treated as objects of wonder, almost like holy relics and were, like ostrich eggs and coconut shells, fitted with mounts of precious metal and displayed on chimneypieces or in special cabinets in well-to-do houses as status symbols. From the late 15th century, detailed depictions of blue and white vessels appear in Italian paintings as precious gifts from the Magi to the Christ Child, such as the little Ming dynasty cup offered by the Magus Caspar in Andrea Mantegna's *Adoration of the Kings* (1500).[5] In *The Feast of the Gods*, begun by Giovanni Bellini in 1514 and finished by Titian in 1526, the gods of Ancient Greece are shown being served a banquet from large Ming dishes.[6]

By the 17th century many of the European maritime powers had set up private companies to trade with the Far East and large cargoes of Chinese porcelain began to arrive in Europe. Thomas Weelkes (1575-1623) wrote poetically if not strictly accurately of

'The Andalusian merchant, that returns
Laden with cochineal and China dishes...'[7]

Much of the porcelain was brought by the ships of the Dutch East India Company and was acquired by the newly prosperous bourgeoisie. These pieces were recorded in the opulent still life paintings of artists such as Osias Beert the Elder (c1580-1623) and later Willem Kalf (c1622-1693). Beert's *Still Life with Nautilus Cup, Fruit, Nuts and Wine* (1610) (fig 2.1, cat F1) is a

Fig 2.1 Osias Beert, *Still Life with Nautilus Cup, Fruit, Nuts and Wine*, 1610. Royal Pavilion & Museums, Brighton & Hove

Fig 2.2 Daniel Marot, Design for a chimneypiece to display Chinese porcelain, c1690

modest display of riches; plentiful fresh fruits, nuts and wine in exquisite glass goblets, a rare nautilus shell in a gilt mount and a Chinese cup filled with mulberries.[8] When Queen Mary II returned from the Netherlands with her Dutch husband, William of Orange, to accede to the English throne, she was already a serious china collector. Her 'vast stock of fine *China*-Ware ... the like whereof was not then to be seen in England' was seen at Hampton Court by Daniel Defoe, who noted that it was displayed 'every Place, where it could be placed, with Advantage'.[9]

Some idea of the overwhelming impact of such displays can be gained from the schemes for interior decoration drawn up by the court architect Daniel Marot (1661-1752), in a series of engravings of ornate chimneypieces all but smothered in porcelain (fig 2.2). It is unknown whether his observations of the displays at Hampton Court influenced Defoe when he came to write the *Farther Adventures of Robinson Crusoe* (1719). Here Crusoe visits China and marvels at a large house, constructed entirely of porcelain,

'... it was a timber house, ... plastered with the earth that makes China ware. The outside, which the sun shone hot upon, was glazed, and looked very well, perfectly white, and painted with blue figures, as the large China ware in England is painted, and hard as if it had been burnt. As to the inside, all the walls, instead of wainscot, were lined with hardened and painted tiles, like the little square tiles we call galley-tiles in England, all made of the finest china, and the figures exceeding fine indeed, with extraordinary variety of colours, mixed with gold, ... the roof was covered with tiles of the same, but of a deep shining black. This was a China ware-house indeed, truly and literally to be called so...' [10]

A number of official customs regulations, authorised by Acts of Parliament, controlled, for a while, the flood of Chinese porcelain imported by the East India Company. Edward IV's Act of 1464, prohibiting the wholesale 'importation of painted wares', was not repealed until 1775, which meant that much porcelain was imported blank and enamelled by English decorators (cat B47). In addition, an Act of 1704 imposed a levy of 12½ per cent on wholesale auction prices of 'porcelain commonly called China-ware or Japanware imported...'. This levy rose to nearly 50 per cent by the 1790s. In addition, the discovery that London china dealers operated a ring to keep auction prices artificially low led the East India Company to discontinue bulk importation.[11]

The Craze for China

The fashion for collecting porcelain, initiated by Queen Mary II, spread rapidly and was dominated by women. The Dehua *blanc-de-chine* porcelains amassed by Sarah Churchill, Duchess of Marlborough, sometime intimate of Queen Anne, were left (after her death in 1744) to John, Duke of Montagu and are now at Boughton House, Northamptonshire. Lady Mary Mordaunt

Fig 2.3 Creamware figure of Zhongliquan, copied from a Chinese original, made in Staffordshire, c1750. Victoria & Albert Museum

(1658-1705), divorced from the Duke of Norfolk, filled Drayton House in Northamptonshire with piles of 'chinaware'. An inventory of her effects includes 'two great china white and blew [sic] rullwagons' (a specific type of Chinese vase).[12] Henrietta Howard (c1688-1767), Countess of Suffolk, mistress of George II, assembled an impressive porcelain collection at Marble Hill House in Twickenham. Lady Elizabeth Montagu (1718-1800), a notable bluestocking, entertained members of her Hill Street salon in her famous 'Chinese room', in the 1750s, surrounded by 'pagodas, nodding mandarins, cushions of Japan satin and curtains decorated by Chinese painting on gauze'.[13] Even Margaret, 2nd Duchess of Portland (1715-1785), better known as a collector of Roman antiquities such as the Portland Vase, had notable, historic, Chinese blue-and-white porcelain that could be seen at Welbeck Abbey in Nottinghamshire until its dispersal in 1786.[14]

Heavy import duties meant that Chinese porcelain remained expensive and relatively scarce throughout much of the 18th century, retaining its allure for collectors. Men and women with smaller disposable incomes had to settle for the new English imitations, which they collected with equal zeal. It was no wonder that writers lampooned their addiction. In *Isabella: or, The Morning* (1740) Sir Charles Hanbury Williams shows the Duchess of Manchester marvelling at a teapot:

'... but see what I have got!
Isn't it a prodigious charming pot?
And ar'n't you vastly glad we made them here?
For Dicky got it out of Staffordshire.
See how the charming vine twists all about!
Lord! what a handle! Jesus! what a spout!
And that old pagod, and that charming child!
If Lady Townsend saw them she'd be wild!'

The retail trade in china was a lucrative business often pursued by respectable women, although their premises could equally well serve as fronts for prostitution. This disturbing ambiguity, associating lust for china with nymphomania in women and effeminacy in men, was demonstrated early in literature.[15] William Wycherley's play, *The Country Wife* (1675) makes play of visits to the china house and women's desire for the product, for, as Lady Fidget says 'we women of quality never think we have China enough'. William Hogarth (1697-1764), highlighted examples of such transgressive behaviour in his paintings and satirical print series. English potters made careful copies of original figures of Chinese gods and sages (fig 2.3, cats B112, B113). An extraordinary assemblage of these figures and vases appears on the mantelpiece in *Tête-à-Tête*, the second of Hogarth's series, *Marriage à la Mode*, painted around 1743 (fig 1.8, cat F6). Here he underlines the moral decadence of the scene in his collection of bizarre Chinese idols (many of

Fig 2.4 William Hogarth, *Southwark Fair*, engraved 1733, detail showing a china stall selling delftware decorated with chinoiseries. Royal Pavilion & Museums, Brighton & Hove

them entirely imaginary), as well as through the more obvious visual references to the dissipated behaviour of the newlyweds.

Commentators such as John Brown, in *An Estimate of Manners and Principles of the Times* (1757), were swift to condemn the fashion for chinoiserie on aesthetic grounds,

'Neither the comic Pencil, nor the serious Pen of our ingenious Countryman [Hogarth], have been able to keep alive the Taste of Nature, or of Beauty. The fantastic and the grotesque have banished both. Every house of fashion is now crowded with Porcelain Trees and Birds, Porcelain Men and Beasts, cross-legged Mandarins and Brahmins, perpendicular lines and stiff right Angles: Every gaudy Chinese Crudity ... is adopted into fashionable Use, and become the Standard of Taste and Elegance'.[16]

Meanwhile, British and European potters applied themselves to discovering the secret of Chinese porcelain, with mixed results. The secret of the recipe for hard-paste porcelain was first cracked at Meissen, near Dresden, where authentic 'true porcelain' was manufactured by 1710 but a dearth of the right ingredients made production elsewhere very difficult.[17] British ceramics at this time were coarse, heavy and brittle. Among valiant British attempts to imitate porcelain was the application of opaque, white tin-glaze to the dark, clay bodies available but this gave only a crude impression of the pale, delicate, Chinese originals. By the mid 17th century, designs of figures and foliage, applied in coloured oxides (especially cobalt blue) crudely approximated to designs noted on Chinese export wares produced largely for the Middle East (see cat B42). These British tin-glazed, 'delftware' vessels are probably the type of ceramics on sale under the collapsing balcony depicted in Hogarth's print *Southwark Fair*, issued in 1733 (fig 2.4). Alternatively, dilute, white clay slip could be poured into relief-carved moulds, fired and glazed with vitrified salt to create saltglazed stoneware, a shiny, resilient material with textural interest, but it was not porcelain.

Eventually technological advances were made at the London factories of Chelsea and Bow, at Longton Hall in Staffordshire and at Derby, when each began producing soft-paste porcelain between 1745 and 1756, having issued a series of patents for the use of methods and materials. They employed a variety of white clays, ground glass and (later) bone ash, to create bone china, the most distinctive and durable English ceramic body of the 19th century and the most economical to produce. Bristol also made soft-paste between 1749-52 before being taken over by the Worcester Porcelain factory.

In 1768 Plymouth pioneered the only British hard-paste porcelain, after William Cookworthy patented the use of Cornish kaolin and *petunse* ('china stone'), both being essential ingredients, but production was short lived. The early factories found it helpful to link their wares with those of China. In 1751 the Worcester factory advertised porcelain of 'Tonquin Manufacture' and the Bristol factory it took over was declared, in 1762, to have been set up

Fig 2.5 Porcelain inkwell, inscribed New Canton, 1750, made at the Bow factory, London. Salisbury & South Wiltshire Museum

in 'in imitation of East India China ware'. Until 1756 the Bow factory called itself 'New Canton', not only because of the style of its products (fig 2.5, cat B50), but also because the factory building itself was said to be modelled on a Cantonese original.[18]

Tea and Fashion

The craze for china in Britain is inextricably linked with the taste for tea and the burgeoning ceramic industry in Britain was greatly stimulated by the need to produce appropriate vessels for serving it. By the mid 18th century china sellers in London and Bath are noted to have stocked tea, coffee and chocolate besides ceramics.[19] The beverage appeared around 1650 (shortly after the arrival of coffee) and was first advertised for sale in the London newspaper *The Gazette*, 2-9 September 1658:

'That Excellent, and by all Physitians approved, China Drink, called by the Chineans, Tcha, by other nations Tay, alias Tee is sold at the Sultaness-head, a Cophee-house...'

Samuel Pepys first tasted it in 1660 and in 1667 he found his wife '... making of Tea ... a drink which Mr Pelling the potticary tells her is good for her colds and difluxions'.[20] Apart from its alleged medicinal properties, one of the great attractions of tea was the varied range of strange and delicate equipment used in its preparation and consumption. Cargoes of bulky but lightweight crates of tea were stabilised by vast amounts of Chinese ceramics, packed below, acting as ballast on the long voyages from China. There were red stoneware pots with spouts and handles (originally used as wine pots by the Chinese but quickly adapted in England to brew the beverage) and tiny cups and plates of thin, white, translucent porcelain, often delicately decorated in blue or in coloured enamels.

Tea drinking provided the gentry and later the aspiring middle classes, with an opportunity to show off their wealth and taste with glamorous imported porcelain. The only alternative material of higher status was silver; ideal for tea urns and kettles, teapots (with insulated handles), jugs, sugar bowls and tea canisters but unsuitable for tea bowls (cups without handles), which became too hot to hold. The hostess of a tea party would bring out her selection of teas, which she kept in canisters stored in a tea chest with several compartments (cat A19). These were kept locked owing to the financial value of the tea. Black teas included flowery or orange pekoe (from 'pak-ho', the downy hairs on the tips of the young buds), pekoe souchong ('sia-chung' meant little plant) and bohea from the Fujian mountains. Green teas included gunpowder, imperial hyson ('yu-tsien', meaning 'before the rains'), singlo or twankay. Many later ceramic canisters were marked helpfully with these names. Thomas Twining set up Tom's coffee-house in Devereux Court in 1706, where he also sold tea; bohea retailed at 16s 0d to 24s 0d and hyson at 14s 0d to 20s 0d per pound.[21]

Fig 2.6 Worcester Porcelain plate, 1770-80, underside, showing imitation Chinese characters. Royal Pavilion & Museums, Brighton & Hove

Until the 19th century, when tea parties became an independent, mid-afternoon activity, the British tea ceremony generally took place after dinner (scheduled around 2pm) when the company parted. Ladies retired to the drawing room to take tea (sometimes served upon a teapoy, a circular table with a central column and tripod feet) while the men continued to drink alcohol before joining them. Tea remained an expensive commodity throughout the 18th century until William Pitt's Commutation Act of 1784 replaced the high excise duties (which often amounted to more than 100 per cent) with a flat tax of 12½ per cent. This had a number of practical effects. Firstly tea lost its exclusive cachet. The government recognised that, after the mid-century horrors of the gin craze 'tea has become an economical substitute to the middle and lower classes of society for malt liquor...'.[22] This meant that tea became a staple drink throughout society and both manufacture and consumption of tea wares grew enormously. Teapots, hitherto of small size, grew much larger and there was a massive increase in production and in varieties of form and decoration of all tea wares, the majority being rather crudely made.

Design sources

The earliest sources for chinoiserie decoration on ceramics probably came from the Netherlands. The Dutch East India Company was importing not only large quantities of Chinese porcelain (from which Queen Mary II could select for her collection) but a wide range of other goods, possibly including figurative textiles, illustrated manuscripts and woodblock prints.[23] In addition to careful copies of Chinese figures, as soon as they could control the application of glazes and enamels, English potters and decorators also imitated Chinese figurative scenes, floral patterns, Buddhist symbols and Chinese characters on to ceramics (fig 2.6, cats B93, B94). Certain motifs gained nicknames; notably 'pagods', the temple-like buildings used by idolaters and by implication, the idols worshipped in them[24] and 'Long Elizas' (a corruption of the Dutch term *lange Lyzen* – long dawdlers or stupids). Other names were adopted unaltered, such as the 'kylin' (qilin), a mythical, hoofed, dog-like dragon that appears in the Worcester porcelain pattern now known as 'Dragons in Compartments' (cat B102), and the 'ho ho bird', ('ho-o' in Japanese), the 'fenghuang' or phoenix that symbolises good fortune.

Fig 2.7 Johan Nieuhof, *An Embassy from the East-India Company*, 1665 p.220 illustration of 'Chinese Priests and Monks'

The first illustrated travel books began to appear in the Netherlands. The *Novus Atlas Sinensis*, by the Jesuit priest, Martino Martini (1614-61), whose maps had fine figurative embellishments, was published in Amsterdam in 1655. This was followed by *An Embassy from the East-India Company, of the United Provinces, to the Grand Tartar Cham or Emperour* [sic] *of China*, by the embassy secretary, Johan Nieuhof (1618-72), in 1665. The first English edition, illustrated by Wenceslaus Hollar and others, was published in London in 1669 and became an important source for decoration on silver as well as delftware and relief-moulded saltglaze vessels from the 1740s onwards. A

Fig 2.8 Lowestoft porcelain bowl painted with detail from Nieuhof, p.220 'Chinese Priests and Monks'. Courtesy Norfolk Museum & Archaeology Service

Fig 2.9 Michel Aubert, engraving after Watteau, *The Goddess Ki Mao Sao*, c1729. John Whitehead Collection

large Lowestoft porcelain punchbowl, for example, is painted in blue with a careful copy of 'Chinese Priests and Monks' from p.220 of Nieuhof's *Embassy...* (figs 2.7, 2.8).[25] A tiny, white saltglaze teapot in the Brighton collection, is moulded with relief images of the Old and Young Viceroys of Canton (cat B16) and a saltglaze tea canister from the British Museum is moulded with tea plants (cat B17), all from Nieuhof's *Embassy...*. The book included over 100 engravings, featuring land and waterscapes, architecture, figure scenes, plants and animals.[26]

Gedenkwaerdige Gesantschappen... (Memorable Missions of the East India Company) (1669) by Olfert Dapper (1639-89), was published in England, confusingly mis-titled *Atlas Chinensis*, in 1671 by the cartographer John Ogilby. Although Dapper never visited China the book contained detailed studies of daily life, religious ceremonial, and native costume and armour. A little later John Stalker and George Parker published their famous *Treatise of Japaning and Varnishing...* (1688). Though more important as a source for decorating furniture, as the title implies, the book's distinctive depiction of buildings with spires and striped roofs can sometimes be found on ceramics.[27]

Around 1710 Watteau (1684-1721) was commissioned to decorate the Cabinet de Roi in the Château de la Muette, a royal hunting lodge in the forest of St Germain, just outside Paris. These decorations constituted one of the earliest European decorative schemes in the chinoiserie style. Although the painted interior was destroyed when Louis XV had the chateau completely rebuilt in 1741, 30 of Watteau's designs were engraved. The engravers included François Boucher and Michel Aubert who, in about 1729, recorded images of two large panels featuring the Chinese goddesses, 'Ki Mao Sao' and 'Thvo Chvu' attended by devoted male worshippers (fig 2.9, cat F4). The careful transcription of names suggests that Watteau may have had access to Chinese source prints. It has been noted that, while Watteau took some care to make the male figures appear suitably exotic with their embroidered robes, droopy moustaches and strange hats, the goddesses themselves resemble capricious Parisian courtesans. The design was copied enthusiastically but ineptly, at London's new Bow porcelain factory around 1752, by the 'Muses modeller' who produced a number of rather lumpy porcelain groups (fig 2.10, cat B116).

François Boucher (1703-70) became the quintessential exponent of the French rococo style. His series of tapestry designs for the Gobelins factory, now preserved at the Musée des Beaux Art at Besançon, established a repertory of chinoiserie subjects and motifs that were widely copied throughout Europe and disseminated to a wider audience through prints by Gabriel Huquier and Pierre Aveline. Together they had a major influence on the modellers and decorators at many of England's porcelain factories. Aveline's engravings of 'Le Feu', and 'La Terre', for example, from Boucher's series of the Four Elements, were copied and applied as early transfer prints to porcelain vessels at the Worcester Factory (fig 2.11, cat B61).

Fig 2.12 After Jean Pillement, *The Ladies Amusement*, pl.148

Boucher also inspired the talented draughtsman and painter, Jean-Baptiste Pillement (1728-1808) who decorated palace interiors all over Europe. Although he executed no scheme in England he spent much of his life there and a number of volumes of his chinoiserie designs were printed in London. The first was the *New Book of Chinese Ornaments* (both drawn and engraved by Pillement) published by Robert Sayer in 1755, followed by several albums engraved by Pierre Canot in 1758-9. He also contributed 900 of the 1,500 illustrations that make up *The Ladies Amusement*, disingenuously subtitled *Whole Art of Japanning Made Easy*, published by Sayer in two editions between 1758 and 1762. This book, which was intended to provide patterns and motifs for decorating not only japanned wares, but also ceramics, enamels, furniture, textiles and silver, proved enormously popular with both amateur and professional painters. Several of the plates are helpfully annotated, eg pl.44 'Romantic rocks form'd by Art to Embellish a Prospect', pl.175 'Painted on Jars or other Large Vessels', or pl.177 'Chinese manner of filling the compartments on their Porcelains &c.'

The copy held at the Victoria & Albert Museum bears the bookplate of William Edkins, the grandson of Michael Edkins, a decorator of Bristol delftware.[28] Motifs and subjects from the book were very widely used by

Fig 2.10 Bow porcelain figure group, the Goddess Ki Mao Sao, c1750-52, Pallant House. Pallant House Gallery, Chichester

Fig 2.11 Worcester porcelain mug, printed with 'Le Feu' after Boucher. The Trustees of the British Museum

British potters to decorate all types of wares, painted and printed. The new technique of transfer-printing was used to produce multiple copies of such designs as 'La Pêche' (Fishing) and 'La Promenade Chinoise', from pl.148 of *The Ladies Amusement* (fig 2.12). They were often combined, printed in blue beneath the glaze on Worcester porcelain mugs in the 1770s (figs 2.13, 2.14, cat B87).[29]

George Edwards and Matthias Darly's *A New Book of Chinese Designs, calculated to Improve the Present Taste* (1754), is notable for its very mannered figures with exaggerated costume detail, which proved attractive to mould makers and decorators in the burgeoning pottery industry. A number of Staffordshire redware teapots and saltglaze tea canisters of the 1760s were applied with relief-moulded figures based on the willowy, long-nailed women and pigtailed boys playing with parrots, that illustrate their book. In addition, the complex scene of a market stall selling haberdashery, enamelled on a Bow porcelain dish of c1765 (cat B78) is closely modelled on pl.32 (fig 2.15).[30]

In the later 18th century the modellers and decorators, over-familiar with the repertory of compositions from existing source books, used their imaginations to extemporise chinoiserie caprices. Some, perhaps, were inspired by the encouragement offered on p.4 of the introduction to *The Ladies Amusement*, 'With Indian and Chinese subjects greater Liberties may be taken, because Luxuriance of Fancy recommends their Productions more than Propriety, for in them is often seen a butterfly supporting an Elephant, or Things equally absurd...' Figures evolved into Europeans wearing fancy dress; coquettish women gliding around gardens carrying sunshades, male servants fishing or playing musical instruments and capering children in oversized pyjamas.

Years later, Charles Lamb went into raptures over the fairytale visions evoked by such examples of 'Old China' (in an essay published in the *London Magazine*, March 1823):

'I love the men with women's faces, and the women, if possible, with still more womanish expressions. Here is a young and courtly Mandarin, handing tea to a lady from a salver ... And here the same lady ... is stepping into a little fairy boat, moored on the other side of this calm garden river .... Farther on – if far or near can be predicated of their world – sea horses, trees, pagodas, ... seen through the lucid atmosphere of fine Cathay ....And now do just look at that merry little Chinese waiter holding an umbrella, big enough for a bed-tester, over the head of that pretty insipid half-Madonna-ish chit of a lady in that very blue summer-house'.

Full-blooded chinoiserie enjoyed a short-lived revival thanks to the taste and patronage of George, Prince of Wales. He visited Barr, Flight and Barr's Worcester porcelain factory in 1807 where he ordered a number of services with opulent designs, richly enamelled and gilt (fig 2.16). Barr, Flight and

Fig 2.13 Worcester porcelain mug, printed with 'La Promenade Chinoise' (above) and 'La Pêche'(below) after Pillement. Worcester Porcelain Museum

Fig 2.14

Fig 2.15 Edwards and Darly, *A New Book of Chinese Designs*, pl.32

Barr also supplied a new range, even more sumptuously decorated, after 1811, when George became Prince Regent (fig 2.17, cat B103). These designs are often described as 'Japan' or 'Imari' (after a trading port in Japan) although they are late caprices on standard chinoiserie motifs.[31] They were almost certainly intended for use at the Marine Pavilion in Brighton, whose first chinoiserie interiors were realised by John and Frederick Crace in 1802-3. The prince also awarded his Royal Warrant to Robert Chamberlain who had set up a new factory at Worcester. Chamberlain created a sumptuous pattern book from which the prince was to select designs (cat B104). He ordered dinner, dessert, tea and breakfast services but could not decide on one design and had every piece decorated in a different pattern. The so-called 'Harlequin' dessert service alone had 190 pieces, including 96 plates and was not delivered until 1811. The total cost of Chamberlain porcelain supplied by 1816 was a staggering £4,047.19s.[32]

In general by 1800, the colourful inhabitants of Cathay had all but disappeared from mass production, leaving gardens with fancy fences and giant chrysanthemums or distant, blue-printed land and waterscapes scattered with trees, boats, birds and pagodas. Of these later patterns, 'Willow' is probably the best known. Around 1790 Josiah Spode adapted a Chinese pattern called 'Mandarin' shortly followed by versions from other factories including Minton and Wedgwood. A variety of Chinese legends were woven together to create a narrative that involved the elopement of a pair of star-crossed lovers from a vengeful father (the Mandarin), who eventually tracks them down. The lovers die but the gods take pity and transform them into birds. The image should contain a weeping willow and a fruit tree, pagodas, figures on a bridge and a pair of flying birds. There are many variants, which have remained in production for over 200 years, the most famous and perhaps the quintessential chinoiserie design.

Stella Beddoe

1 From *Isabella: or, The Morning* (1740) by Sir Charles Hanbury Williams
2 See Rose Kerr, 'Chinese Porcelain in early European Collections' in *Encounters: the Meeting of Asia and Europe*, ed. Jackson and Jaffer, V&A, 2004 pp.46-7
3 *porceletta* derives from Latin for 'little pig', referring to the rounded shape of the cowry shell. Kerr suggests that, well into the 17th century, many in England believed that porcelain was made from pulverised seashells.
4 *The Travels of Marco Polo*, translated by Hugh Murray, London, 1845, p.203 see www.books.google.co.uk
5 J Paul Getty Museum, Malibu, California, Cat. No 85.PA.417
6 National Gallery of Art, Washington DC, Cat No 1942.9.1
7 'Thule, the Period of Cosmography'; the merchants were Portuguese rather than Spanish.
8 The cup dates from the reign of Wan Li (1573-1619) during the Ming Dynasty. Brighton & Hove Museums, Cat No FA000061
9 From Defoe's *Tour thro' the Whole Island of Great Britain* (1724-29) quoted by Hilary Young, *English Porcelain 1745-95*, V&A, London, 1999, p.184
10 Daniel Defoe, *Farther Adventures of Robinson Crusoe*, 1719, see www.books.google.co.uk

Fig 2.16 Worcester porcelain plate, enamelled and gilt with chinoiserie designs for George, Prince of Wales, 1807-08. Worcester Porcelain Museum

Fig 2.17 Worcester porcelain plate, enamelled and gilt with chinoiserie designs for the Prince Regent, 1811-12. Worcester Porcelain Museum

11 Young, op.cit., p.74-5
12 See Tessa Murdoch ed. *Noble Households, Eighteenth Century Inventories of great English houses...*, Cambridge, 2006
13 See Elizabeth Eger, 'Bluestocking Culture Displayed', Luxury in the Eighteenth Century, ed. Maxine Berg and Eger, Basingstoke, Hampshire, 2003, p.193
14 Oliver Impey, *Porcelain for Palaces*, London, 1990, p.68-69
15 See David Beevers's discussion (in this catalogue, p.14) of references to china-women in the plays of Ben Jonson in the early 1600s.
16 Quoted by Sarah Richards, *Eighteenth century Ceramics, products for a civilised society*, Manchester, 1999, p.178
17 For a highly readable account of this endeavour see Janet Gleeson, *The Arcanum, The Extraordinary True Story of the Invention of European Porcelain*, London, 1998
18 Young, op.cit., p.85
19 Richards, op.cit., p.60
20 Quoted by Robin Emmerson, *British Teapots and Tea Drinking, 1700-1850*, HMSO, London, 1992, p.1-2. He points out that, since the British East India Company had its headquarters in Amoy, we have always used the Fujian dialect word 'tea' rather than the Cantonese 'cha'.
21 Ibid. p.3-4
22 Ibid. p.10
23 See Perrin Stein, op.cit., (note 14, p.25)1996, pp.601-02, who demonstrates that François Boucher made extensive use of original Chinese woodblock prints for his chinoiserie compositions.
24 Defined in Diderot's *Encyclopédie*, 1765, quoted in Danièlle Kisluk-Grosheide, 'The Reign of the Magots and Pagods', *Metropolitan Museum Journal*, Vol 37, New York, 2002, p.177
25 Inscribed 'Elizath Buckle, 1768', at the Castle Museum, Norwich.
26 For a full discussion of the uses of see Leslie Grigsby, 'Johan Nieuhoff's *Embassy:...*' in *The Magazine Antiques*, New York, Jan 1993, pp.172-83
27 For instance on a large Bow porcelain tureen at Pallant House, see Gabszewicz and Freeman, *Bow Porcelain*, London,1982, item No.75, p.60-61, illustrated pl.V
28 Note in the introduction to the facsimile (published1966) of the copy of the 1762 edition, held at the Victoria & Albert Museum.
29 See Branyan, French & Sandon, *Worcester Blue and White Porcelain*, 1751-1790, London, 1989, item II.A.10, p.313. One rare mug, ibid. item II.B.7, p.334 also includes the design 'Temple Bells', which first appears on the title page of the *New Book of Chinese Ornaments* and was later included on pl.37 of *The Ladies Amusement*.
30 The source was identified by Bernard Watney, *English Ceramic Circle Transactions*, London, Vol.8 pt.2, 1972, pp213-23, pl.173. Young notes that a copy of Edwards and Darly's book was found among the papers of John Bowcock, clerk to the Bow porcelain company, Young, op.cit., discussing Pl.XXVII, p.208.
31 Such terms are confusing; Imari is most helpfully used to describe rich designs primarily in red, blue and gold, often with textile sources, rather than specific to Japan or China.
32 John Sandon, *Dictionary of Worcester Porcelain, Vol. 1*, Woodbridge, Suffolk, 1993, p.269

Chinoiserie Silver in Britain

Fig 3.1 Chinese porcelain bowl, Wanli period, c.1580, with silver-gilt mounts. The Burghley House Collection

Fig 3.2 Chocolate cup and saucer cover, gold, maker's mark only stuck four times, c.1685. Flat chased with chinoiserie figures, birds and flowers. Leeds Museums & Galleries (Temple Newsam)

Early Years

One of the main tasks of the gold and silversmiths' trade has always been to demonstrate the wealth, status and fashion-consciousness of its clients. From time immemorial objects made of precious metals have been among the first to reflect changes in taste and style by the adaptation of their shapes and decoration to accord with the latest trends in fashion. Thus it might be expected that the exotic and luxurious imports from the Far East, so sought after in the early Age of Exploration, might have influenced the work of contemporary English goldsmiths. But, possibly because little Chinese and Japanese silversmiths' work reached Europe until the later 17th century (with the possible exception of filigree) there is almost no evidence to suggest any Far Eastern influence. The classical tradition held sway almost entirely. Instead, influences from the East came from Islamic design, in the form of engraved decoration of 'arabesques' and 'mauresques': stylised floral decoration contained within borders and geometric panels which can be seen on almost every kind of silver object from communion cups to tankards at any date between the mid 16th and mid 17th centuries.

The first contact of the English goldsmiths with the arts of China and the Far East probably came with the orders for the mounting of imported porcelain vessels. With the establishment of Macau as a trading station by the Portuguese in 1557 porcelain and other goods could now be shipped to Europe regularly. In England their continued rarity called for the blue and white bowls, boxes, ewers and basins to be enhanced (or 'trimmed') by silver and silver-gilt mounts, sometimes of great sophistication. Yet these mounts show almost no awareness of the decoration on the vessels which they are intended to frame and augment. At their finest, such as the ewer and basin formerly at Burghley, now in the Metropolitan Museum of Art, they use an elegant combination of motifs derived from the full Mannerist repertoire. The Wanli period blue and white bowl from Burghley, reputedly presented by Queen Elizabeth to her godchild Sir Thomas Walsingham (fig 3.1), has plain straps and a lip-band with scrolling tendrils of semi-formalised flowers and leaves. To represent the much larger quantities of porcelain that arrived after c1600 and which was subsequently mounted, there is the square-sectioned teapot or wine vessel with its gilt handle, collar, chain and spout – stopper from c1640 (cat B44).

Fig 3.3 Salver. Birmingham Museums & Art Gallery

The Restoration: 'huge Vasas of wrought plate'

It was not until the Restoration of Charles II in 1660, which brought with it a sea-change in attitudes to luxury led by the court, that the goldsmiths had enough confidence to begin experimenting and developing new styles to satisfy their clients' voracious appetite for opulence. Oriental themes (described vaguely as 'Japan', 'China' or 'India work') became hugely popular. For the showy new lacquer or japanned cabinets the goldsmiths supplied garnitures of highly embossed silver vases, beakers and bottles to surmount them, no doubt derived from examples seen in Holland.[1] These imitate the same forms in Chinese and Japanese porcelain and could be arranged in similar ways in suites of twos, threes, fives, or sevens (and no doubt re-arranged according to whim). Like so much that is associated with chinoiserie, they were to be found in the luxurious private apartments of courtesans and profligate women. Evelyn was astonished at them in the Countess of Arlington's dressing room at Goring House in 1673 ('silver jarrs and vasas') and ten years later in the Duchess of Portsmouth's apartment ('huge Vasas of wrought plate'),[2] while contemporary inventories describe them as 'jarrs', 'beekers', 'perfume potts', and 'flower potts'.[3] Their production appears to have peaked before 1680 although later examples are known.[4]

Despite the oriental shapes of these vessels, their high relief embossed decoration is entirely European: generally they use festoons and swags of naturalistic fruits, flowers and leaves. One group (epitomised by the highly sophisticated goldsmiths Thomas Jenkins and Jacob Bodendeich) has characteristic trailing classical acanthus leaves, sometimes with amorini, and clearly derive from continental sources.[5] Objects from this group appear in the vanitas still life paintings of Pieter Gerritsz Van Roestraten, the Dutch-born artist working in London from the 1660s. A second group of mainly unmarked pieces at Knole,[6] Welbeck (cat A3), the Untermyer Collection[7] and those formerly at Belton,[8] employ vertical lobes or fluting and three-dimensional swags of fruit around the necks as unifying motifs.

'Japan work' for Ladies' Bedrooms and Male Conviviality

In contrast to these high-relief embossed vases there is an exceptionally interesting three-piece garniture at Belvoir Castle (not available for the exhibition)[9] which is decorated with flat-chased scenes of improbable Chinese figures, exotic birds and plants. This introduces us to the first uniquely English contribution to European chinoiserie: the vogue (for a time almost a craze) for this distinctive form of decoration on objects associated either with ladies' bedrooms and dressing rooms (and the *levées* which took place within them), or with pieces used for male celebration and conviviality.[10] Included in this exhibition from the former group are a pair of gilt salvers (possibly *gantières* or merely useful stands) (fig 3.3, cat A1), a pair of snuffers and its stand (cat A4), and Lady Derby's chocolate cup and saucer (the beverage being served in dressing rooms for breakfast) (fig 3.2,

Fig 3.4 The Mildmay Monteith, silver, maker's mark for George Garthorne, London, 1684-5. Ashmolean Museum, Oxford

cat A7). For men there are the two-handled cup (cat A6), a tankard (cat A8) and two monteiths (used for rinsing wine glasses but also – after removing their notched rims – as punch bowls (fig 3.4, cat A5, A11).[11]

In 1992 Philippa Glanville suggested that there were over 250 objects or groups decorated in this style, including some 30 toilet services or parts, and many more will have come to light since then.[12] They date between 1679 and 1697 although the great majority are from the 1680s.[13] The work of some of the most esteemed goldsmiths of the day, as well as many run-of-the-mill craftsmen, can be found in this style: for toilet services William Fowle,[14] Robert Smythier,[15] Anthony Nelme, Jacob Bodendeich, Ralph Leake, and Thomas Jenkins. Some of these also made drinking equipment, but other makers include John Duck, George Garthorne, Robert Cooper, Benjamin Pyne as well as goldsmiths from York, Newcastle, Hull, Barnstaple and Dublin.[16] But it would be a mistake to look for anything distinctive in the work of these individual goldsmiths: the shapes and forms of the objects themselves are generally predictable. Rather, the most interesting work here is that of the specialist chaser - either a sub-contractor in a nearby workshop or one employed in-house - to whom the completed object would have been supplied for its final decoration. How then can this craze be accounted for, who were the craftsmen, and from where – if anywhere - did they obtain their sources?

The technique of flat chasing superficially resembles engraving, but involves compressing or moving the metal in lines to achieve the desired pictorial effect (and not by removing the metal as in engraving). It is therefore a more sculptural process and perhaps more suitable for a craftsman's freehand inventiveness in design than the more contrived two-dimensional linearity of engraving. The chinoiserie scenes of the 1680s are intended to amuse and delight with their spontaneous and witty evocations of the East rather than impress with complex heraldry or learned inscriptions which were the staple fare of engravers at this time. The chinoiseries were meant to be enjoyed in the relatively informal surroundings of dressing rooms or parlours rather than in formal spaces such as great halls or saloons. Much of their effect has a cartoon-like quality that is entirely deliberate and might be lost in the more precise delineation of engraving. It was a style that appealed at all social levels: from the Countess of Exeter with her 'Dressing Plate Japann'd' or Lady Derby with her gold chocolate cup, down to the tradesmen of small provincial towns with their silver mugs and cups.

If the goldsmiths themselves were not responsible for the decoration of these objects then who was? The sheer number of surviving pieces and their widely varying quality have led to a consensus that there may have been more than one specialist workshop, or at least a number of different hands working in one or more different establishments.[17] But no firm evidence or names have been discovered to flesh out this mysterious world. The connoisseur can only surmise whether the chaser who used the 'architectural' features on the toilet salvers

Fig 3.5 Detail from a 'View of Hanchieu', from Arnoldus Montanus, *Atlas Chinensis*... 1671 This is a possible source for the ubiquitous mustachioed figure either holding a parasol or being shielded by one and who appears on many flat chased chinoiserie silver pieces during the 1680s. The Brotherton Library, University of Leeds

(fig3.3, cat A1), that suggest the fabled Great Wall of China or maybe a scene from a play with an exotic theme, can be the same craftsman who decorated the famous Brownlow tankards with similar features.[18] Certain motifs have been suggested as 'signatures' for a particular workshop: the sun peeping from behind clouds, seen on both the Mildmay and Erdigg monteiths (cat A5, A11); this is also found on other finely decorated objects but with different makers' marks.[19] The decorator of these two monteiths also shows his figures generally standing astride boulders or rocks; each contains one panel with a figure gesticulating towards either an idol or a 'dog of fo'. On the other hand these features could merely reflect a common printed design source.[20]

What are these sources? Western ideas of China and its appearance had long been formed by the many literary descriptions of travellers, from Marco Polo onwards, until Johan Nieuhof's *Embassy* appeared in 1665 (English translation 1669) as the first illustrated account. This provided a remarkable panorama of the empire with engraved plates depicting its topography, flora and fauna, as well as its inhabitants and their customs. This book and the subsequent *Atlas Chinensis* (1671), published under the name Arnoldus Montanus, but in fact by Olfert Dapper, provided a rich quarry of potential imagery for artists' imaginations into the middle of the next century. Additional source material was also at hand in the decoration seen on luxury export goods - lacquer cabinets and coromandel screens, porcelain, and textiles. The difference between the two was of course that the European topographers showed China through western eyes by using 'correct' linear perspective, something entirely foreign to the Chinese tradition where figures and buildings are shown as if floating in a world of dream-like unreality.

Nevertheless direct quotations either from publications or from export products are quite rare, since the chasers, or those supplying them with patterns, preferred to adapt the sources for their own purposes. Even so there are some obvious derivations, for example the ubiquitous moustachioed pot-bellied warrior, with one hand on his hip, either holding or being shaded by a parasol (fig 3.4, cat A5, see fig 3.5). Another frequently encountered exotic figure wears a vast overhanging feathered hat. He turns out to be a mendicant who first appears seated with his legs crossed in Nieuhof's *Embassy*. Yet he is clearly one of the parade of outrageously be-hatted gentlemen on the Erdigg monteith (cat A11).[21] (Boucher was later to transform him into a virtuoso soloist in *La Danse chinoise*.[22]) Yet another is a coolie, seen on Lady Derby's cup, balancing parcels over his shoulder similar to another in Montanus's *Atlas*. The figures of birds and plants are similarly repeated with imaginative variations.

Thus the lack of precise visual quotations from these publications makes it more likely that the chasers acquired their knowledge at secondhand, perhaps through the small number of 'pattern drawers' who provided designs for a variety of different craftsmen, notably for needle workers both professional and amateur.[23] At least nine were listed in London poll tax documents of

1692.[24] Evidence of their employment by goldsmiths may be found in the inventory of William Fowle, a noted supplier of 'Japan work' toilet services, whose shop contained 'silver patternes' in 1684.[25]

Other examples of the work of pattern drawers using either the publications or imported goods as source material can be seen, for example, in the embroidery on the jacket (cat D1) with chinoiserie figurative stitching. Indeed the unusual 'stitched' or 'stabbed' effect of the chasing on the silver objects of this period may be a deliberate attempt to imitate such embroidery. Similarly Vanderbank tapestries (cat D2) were designed by professional draughtsmen looking to a combination of sources from travel books to Mughal miniatures probably intending to create the effect of coromandel screens with their determined absence of western rules of perspective. But there are other sources which must have come to hand reasonably easily for the professionals working for the luxury trades at this time. One does not have to look far to find references to Chinese and Japanese porcelain. Examples include the lady in the kimono with her small dog and the child frightening a small bird on the snuffer stand (cat A4). Other sources are entirely western - exotic fountains, ruined classical architecture, and the flora and fauna of the English countryside can often be found in curious juxtaposition.[26] The influence of the contemporary stage and the popularity of plays with an oriental theme have also been suggested as sources.

The Influence of Chinese Export Silver

By the 1680s Chinese silversmiths' work was beginning to arrive in the west. Newly opened mines in Central and South America resulted in great quantities of bullion being exported to China by Europeans in exchange for luxury goods. Finished silver objects were then exported to Europe either as ornamental objects such as the two-handled cup, cover and stand in the Royal Collection (cat A10) or as tea or coffee pots and bowls, the earliest dated example being the teapot with marks added in London in 1682.[27] The decoration of these objects often took the form of reserve panels, with cast and chased scenes of branches of pine, bamboo and prunus, birds, deer being pursued by huntsmen, or figures crossing bridges. Similar features also appear in low-relief carved lacquer boxes and it is typical of *sawasa*, a form of metalwork made from copper alloy with black lacquer (which in its turn was imitating Japanese models).[28] The small hexagonal jar, dating from c1680 (cat A17), may originally have been part of a garniture but was evidently transformed into a teapot by the addition of a spout and handle some 70 years later. Chinese export filigree silver, including toilet sets, tea equipage and jewellery, was also especially prized and imitated in the west.[29]

Somewhat more faithful imitations of Chinese originals were soon being produced by London goldsmiths, especially small private objects for personal use. The Albert Collection contained a remarkable group of small scent bottles of different shapes[30] including an example close to a design by

Fig 3.6 Box, silver, maker's mark only, c.1680. Cast and chased with figures in a landscape. Victoria & Albert Museum

C de Moelder published in 1694[31] and a snuff box similar to fig 3.6, cat A2, which is inscribed as the gift of King Charles II to his mistress Nell Gwynn. Slightly later there appear a group of small cups combining these characteristic floral chinoiserie panels with entirely European caryatid handles, the effect of which is to create a charming stylistic solecism.[32]

The shapes of Chinese vessels continued to exercise a fascination and inspiration for English goldsmiths not least for the new cult of tea, coffee and chocolate drinking. The ginger jar shape, becoming more ovoid in profile, became popular for coffee pots once the Turkish-inspired conical topped vessel had lost favour; it merely required the addition of a curved spout and handle at right angles. A small tea kettle from Burghley (cat A12) is, in effect, a compressed hexagonal ginger jar with a swing handle and multi-chinned spout. The sides have six reserve panels with 'Indian' or 'Persian' figures of befeathered horsemen and hunters in landscapes. It is a variation on the lacquer or *sawasa*-inspired objects with somewhat less obvious Chinese scenes: here the figures may once again be derived from travel books.[33] Chinese melon-shaped wine pots were briefly adapted for some of the earliest teapots (cat A9). But by the turn of the century teapots became either pear-shaped or globular, neither shape entirely suggestive of the East or strictly speaking 'chinoiserie'. For tea bowls, for drinking the beverage itself, the goldsmiths were at an obvious disadvantage because the metal was such a good conductor of heat that they were virtually impossible to hold. Nevertheless a few silver tea bowls and saucers are known, some en suite with basins, with radiating flutes and scalloped borders based on contemporary porcelain 'chrysanthemum' dishes (cat A13). Indeed, if only subliminally, Chinese influence was to permeate the design of borders for whole groups of bowls, dishes (including 'strawberry' dishes), salvers and waiters well into the middle of the 18th century. For example the ubiquitous scalloped-shaped 'Bath border', one of the most popular early-to mid 18th century patterns, can be seen on Ding-ware porcelain dishes from at least the 11th century.[34]

Rococo chinoiserie Silver

Apart from this, chinoiserie decoration disappeared almost entirely from the products of the London goldsmiths soon after the beginning of the new century. The reason may be the almost total adoption of the French baroque style under the influence of the Huguenot goldsmiths who increasingly commanded the field. There was no room for chinoiserie in their repertoire despite its continued - albeit subdued - presence in other areas of the luxury trades including ceramics, textiles and furniture. Thus it was not until after the popular success of the French Jesuit Jean-Baptiste Du Halde's *Description of the Empire of China* in 1736 that the public imagination was once again re-ignited and chinoiserie re-appeared as a popular alternative to contemporary classicism, alongside the 'modern' (ie rococo) style. Shortly afterwards it was to be joined by gothic, to make a trio of options available to the person of taste.

For silver, however, there is a curious double paradox to note, for although the first generation of Huguenot goldsmiths had eschewed chinoiserie it was the second generation who were responsible for its emergence and flowering from the 1740s onwards. Secondly, although many of the design sources came from France it appears that very little chinoiserie silver was ever made in continental Europe (or has not survived).[35] Yet, to complete the conundrum, one of the most spectacular pieces of chinoiserie silver in this exhibition, the centrepiece of 1747 by Claude Ballin II (cat A15), was evidently made for an English client, Sir Gilbert Heathcote.

In the 17th century chinoiserie silver had been found in the domestic spaces of both men and women, but in this rococo phase, with its principal use among items for tea and coffee drinking and for informal dining, its association is mainly with women since it was generally to be found in their drawing rooms and dressing rooms, garden pavilions and supper rooms. It goes without saying that chinoiserie silver can only be fully understood and enjoyed within the architectural and aesthetic context of the time – supremely in the Chinese Room at Claydon, or the Birdcage Room at Grimsthorpe where

'the thought of man is not restrained within the limits of nature and reality, and that, to form monsters and join incongruous shapes and appearances cost the imagination no more trouble than to conceive the most natural and familiar objects'.[36]

The 'modern' style (that is, French-inspired naturalistic rococo – *le style pitturesque*) had already reached its apogee when the leading goldsmiths adopted chinoiserie. They were no doubt spurred on by their clients' appetite for new fashions and also inspired by the new engraved ornamental prints appearing from France. Tea canisters and equipages – small but expensive essentials for any lady of taste – led the way. Lewis Pantin's first tentative step appears in 1739, when he added a dragon's head to the handle of a sugar box otherwise entirely encrusted with *rocaille* ornament.[37] Three years later Paul de Lamerie adapted his standard elegant canister design to incorporate the cast heads of negroes and chinamen and women among naturalistic foliage on the sides in a set at Nottingham Castle Museum.

Early rococo ornamental prints, specifically intended for craftsmen including goldsmiths, chasers and engravers, were appearing in London by the mid 1730s. Some included chinoiseries - for example, Jacques de Lajoue's *Receuil Nouveau de differens Cartouches* (circa 1734) which was known in England by 1737 and subsequently published in a pirated edition.[38] Its depiction of a storm-tossed ship with a dragon at its prow was used by Nicolas Sprimont on the tea kettle for the future Catherine the Great's Oranienbaum service (1745). Home-grown sources for chinoiserie appeared from 1741 with Francis Vivares's edition of William de la Cour's *First Book of Ornament*.[39]

These printed design sources were obviously important but should not be overstated. The English goldsmiths were more than capable of using their own inventive skills to develop a unique version of chinoiserie, with only the occasional hint of a debt to an outside source. A popular and highly appropriate early motif was the tea-picker or cane-cutter (fig 3.7, cat A16), loosely inspired by plates in Nieuhof's *Embassy* of 70 years earlier, and developed by de Lamerie for tea canisters from at least 1744. The angular sides of the rectangular box have been softened, helmeted Chinese-looking putti stare out from each corner, and in the main panels a sugar cane cutter is working under a palm tree. The design was plagiarised and used by a large number of different makers (with varying degrees of success) for over 100 years.[40]

The asymmetrical shaped cartouches framing the panels on this canister and its variants by de Lamerie are some of the most completely fortuitous rococo ornaments in the entire English repertoire. For some 15 years similar cartouches were used by his contemporaries and successors to frame an endless variety of figurative chinoiserie scenes on canisters, teapots (cat A20) coffee pots and urns (cat A21). Often they show Chinese figures seated at table drinking tea or wine, walking in the landscape with parasols, gathering in the harvest, or standing at ease and smoking. The panels are either cast and chased, or embossed and chased, or, in some later cases, die-stamped and chased. Teapots, although inexplicably rare, tend to be ovoid, coffee pots and tea urns (or 'vases') are pear shaped, and tea kettles – some of the most virtuoso of the whole period – are often melon shaped. Canisters are frequently *bombé* in shape, or rectangular with pagoda style canopied covers. A most interesting small group contains extremely crowded scenes, jumbling figures and architecture with a complete lack of recession or depth (cat A19). It has been suggested that their decoration derives from Huet's schemes at Chantilly, or from the engravings after Peyrotte or Mondon.[41] Another source might be Lajoue's fantastical series *Prosternation, Observation, Divertissement and Conversation chinois.*[42]

From about 1760 there is a subtle and interesting change. In particular the figurative decoration on coffee pots and tea urns, hitherto confined within shaped panels framed by cartouches and often cast, now begins to spread all over the body of vessels which are invariably embossed and chased. At the same time their shapes become taller and more attenuated and frequently double *bombé*. These features allow the virtuoso chaser more space to deploy his skills which often achieve a remarkable depth of relief. Whether there is just a single master craftsman or workshop involved is unknown, but comparisons between many different examples reveal a wide disparity of quality. Some names have been suggested including Christopher Heckel, a cousin of the chaser of gold boxes Augustin Heckel, whose signature is found on a pair of plaques at the Victoria & Albert Museum. Others are Daniel Gaab and the Norwegians Emick and John Christopher Romer.[43]

Fig 3.7 Tea Canister, silver-gilt, maker's mark for Paul de Lamerie, London, 1747-8. Once one of a pair. Embossed, cast and chased with chinoiseries. The Worshipful Company of Goldsmiths

Fig 3.8 Coffee Pot, silver, maker's mark for Francis Crump, London, 1769. Leeds Museums & Galleries (Temple Newsam)

Makers' marks appearing on these distinctive items include those of William Plummer, William Grundy, the Smith and Sharp and Whipham and Wright partnerships. A fine example from 1769 from Temple Newsam by Francis Crump includes a pierced foot – a feature which only appears on this craftsman's work (fig 3.8, cat A24). Two of the three figurative scenes on this pot are taken directly from the designs of Jean Pillement (fig 3.9) whose work became a hugely popular source on silver and ceramics especially after many of his chinoiserie vignettes were published in Robert Sayer's *The Ladies Amusement* in at least two editions between 1758 and 1762.[44] A cast finial in the form of a seated chinaman is also found on pots by several of the makers of this period.

Tea Tubs, Dragons and Pagoda-epergnes

Jean Pillement was also the source of the engraved decoration on a number of 'tea tubs' – both cube-shaped (cat A27) and ovoid - which became one of the most popular forms for tea canisters of the 1760s and 1770s. The cube versions were deliberate imitations of the tea chests in which the tea was imported into England. They often have imitation Chinese calligraphic characters engraved on their sides as an alternative to pictorial scenes or armorials.[45] Sometimes their borders consist of trailing flowers, or alternatively a Chinese fret pattern.

Although these canisters bear the marks of several different goldsmiths they appear nevertheless to have been the virtual monopoly of Parker and Wakelin, one of the leading retailers of the time whose ledgers show that they were either commissioned specially for their clients or sometimes for stock.[46] They retailed at about £8.10s.0d each. The example illustrated (fig 3.10) was bought by Colonel Sir Paul Pechell in 1767, and may have been one of a pair (possibly contained within a box, either japanned, or made of shagreen or ivory). Parker and Wakelin's favourite engraver was Robert Clee whose own *Book of Eighteen Leaves* had appeared as long ago as 1737.[47]

There is every reason to believe that engravers particularly enjoyed using the chinoiserie style as it provided unrivalled opportunities for them to demonstrate their skills (and thereby make higher charges for fashion). The real flowering comes between 1750 and 1765 when some truly virtuoso work can be seen on a number of salvers with large flat areas left blank for appropriate decoration and sometimes with borders incorporating cast chinoiserie heads or pagodas. Some of the elaborate cartouches surrounding the armorial devices have affinities with engraved furniture designs (especially for looking glasses) by Thomas Chippendale (1754 and 1762, engraved by Matthias Darly), Thomas Johnson (1758) and Ince and Mayhew (1762). Figures standing in garden buildings with upswept eaves, altars with a seated joss, winged dragons, ho ho birds and flowers are combined for astonishing effects.[48]

Chinese shapes continued to exercise a subliminal fascination on the design for dishes and tureens for the dining table. Their covers sometimes appear with finials suggestive of pagoda canopies (including a service supplied to

Fig 3.9 Plate from Jean Pillement's *Etudes de differentes figures Chinoises inventées et desinées par J. Pillement…*

Chippendale and Adam's neo-classical dining room at Harewood[49]) and *The Ladies Amusement* provided some improbable designs.[50] But Sir Gilbert Heathcote was less covert in his taste by ordering his French surtout from the great Claude Ballin II with its two winged dragons from whose mouths emanate great fiery flames, from which in turn emerge the candles to illuminate the table. His *surtout* was presumably for use at night, for supper rather than dinner, when an eye-catcher was needed for the centre of the table as well as a source of artificial light.[51] Similar dragons can be found as far back as the late 17th century on the handles of a covered tureen in a painting of an imaginary buffet by Desportes now in the Metropolitan Museum of Art.[52] At almost the same time the Somerset baronet Sir Thomas Champneys was likewise inspired to order a pair of sauce boats whose handles take the form of winged dragons who stare down angrily and are about to breath fire into the bowl (cat A14). In the absence of any marks this extraordinary piece of modelling has been attributed in the past to the Kandler workshop, although there is good reason to suppose it to be the work of James Shruder.[53]

Sir Gilbert's *surtout* was a forerunner of one of the most delightful of all the manifestations of late rococo chinoiserie, the pagoda-canopied epergne (fig 3.11, cat A25). Early table centrepieces, with interchangeable tureens and dishes, candle sconces, cruets and casters, had given way to lighter stands for different sized baskets and dishes intended for dessert fruits and sweetmeats. A design by William Kent published in 1744 introduced the idea of an open-work canopy in the form of a garden arbour. From here it was but a short step before the canopies turned 'Chinese'. By the early 1750s their 'roofs' acquired upturned eaves and bells, the piercing of the swing-handled baskets started to resemble Chinese railings while the leafy branches became 'spiky' and oriental, and with the occasional surprise of a mandarin's head to be seen on the hinges or joints. By the late 1750s epergnes were being sold in considerable numbers by Parker and Wakelin who employed Thomas Pitts as their specialist supplier.[54]

These pieces are surely related (however freely) to the designs for 'Chinese' garden arbours and pavilions of William Halfpenny and others.[55] Indeed it is not too fanciful to imagine them being used in these locations for desserts or suppers especially in conjunction with a service of Chelsea or Worcester porcelain sporting a chinoiserie pattern. In China itself Sir William Chambers had admired the '[garden] buildings adapted to the recreations of each particular time of the day'.[56] Thus an imaginary *fête* in the *jardin anglo-chinois* might be accompanied also by wine bottles contained in galleried coasters, and glass-lined open-work salt cellars and mustard pots suggestive of 'Chinese fret' or railings. Chippendale supplied many pages of designs for these in the *Director,* equally suitable for the galleries of tea tables (cat C14) or for goldsmiths' work. He also supplied designs for candlestands supported by chinamen, an echo of which can be seen in a set of silver sticks made for Sir Crisp Gascoyne by Phillips Garden in 1756, to be copied, with variations, in the Regency (cat A30).[57]

Fig 3.10 Tea Canister ('Tea Tub'), silver, makers' marks for Aaron and Louis Lestourgeon, London, 1771. Retailed by Parker and Wakelin. Engraved with Chinese calligraphic characters. Leeds Museums & Galleries (Temple Newsam)

The Duke of Sussex (1773-1843), whose epergne of 1761 is one of the highlights of the exhibition, was one of the younger brothers of King George IV and no doubt a frequent guest and admirer of the unique chinoiserie decorations of the Royal Pavilion. Perforce he must have acquired his epergne secondhand and this might well reflect his own more measured and antiquarian taste than his elder brother's.[58] Indeed, apart from the extravagancies of the Pavilion, the third phase of English chinoiserie silver, corresponding to the Regency period, is partly characterised by a more accurate and scholarly interpretation of original Chinese models.

Chinoiserie Silver in the Regency

Chinoiserie and early neo-classicism made awkward bedfellows (although Chippendale found a *modus vivendi* for his clients notably at Nostell and Harewood) so it is not surprising that the former went into eclipse between c1780 and c1810. But some interesting developments around this latter date augured well for yet another revival of chinoiserie in silver. On the one hand Charles Heathcote Tatham in his influential book *Designs for Ornamental Plate* (1806) now advocated a return to massiveness and archaeological accuracy, while George Smith in *Household Furniture* (1808) included views of interiors in the Chinese style among his heady eclectic mix. By now there was a far more informed knowledge of the East, while underscoring everything was the prevailing spirit of romantic antiquarianism. Thus in 1810 Paul Storr appears to have inaugurated a new vogue for copies (or close adaptations) of Chinese originals when he made a near exact twin to an octagonal Chinese bowl and cover, with cast panels of prunus, flowers, birds and pagodas, and en suite matching stands.[59] Chinese export silver, whose basic style had scarcely changed in the course of over a century, provided the model for the short-lived fashion which followed.[60] William Beckford was an extremely sensitive connoisseur of style and himself designed (possibly with Gregorio Franchi) a number of exquisite adaptations from a wider range of original Chinese models (cat A28, A29).

For the fashionable world of the immediate post-Waterloo years the 18th century rococo style (including chinoiserie) was a welcome reminder of the splendours of the *ancien régime* and it was adopted with gusto. At the same time, often because of their more expansive lifestyles, families were increasingly choosing to augment their inherited 18th century plate by adding matching new items, for example to their chinoiserie tea equipment, or extending sets of candlesticks (fig 3.12, cat A30), or enhancing 18th century original designs (cat A31). The difference between the original and the revivals is clear enough to see; the latter are usually bigger in scale, more robust in decoration and coarser in execution.

It seems extraordinary that George IV for all his love of chinoiserie never encouraged a revival of this style for the Grand Service of plate which he built up over the Regency and during his own reign. His spectacular chinoiserie dining room at the Royal Pavilion, with its massive dragon chandelier, should have been the setting for a whole new trend in design for plate. Instead, the Regency period saw a more modest development of the style: new shapes and decoration for tea canisters, and a small group of delightful taper sticks in the form of standing chinamen.[61] But, starved of royal patronage, by the time Queen Victoria ascended the throne chinoiserie had once again ceased to be a mainstream style for the goldsmiths and their clients.

James Lomax

Fig 3.11 Epergne, silver, maker's mark for Thomas Pitts, London, 1761. Engraved with the arms of HRH the Duke of Sussex, the brother of George IV. Private collection

1 See the discussion on silver furniture in Gordon and Philippa Glanville, 'A la cour des Stuarts', in exhibition catalogue *Quand Versailles etait meuble de l'argent*, Versailles (2007-8).

2 [April 14 1673] '...her new dressing roome at Goring House, where was a bed, 2 glasses, silver jarrs and vasas, cabinets and so rich furniture...[Oct 4 1683]...Japon Cabinets, Skreenes, Pendule Clocks, huge Vasas of wrought plate, Tables, Stands, Chimny furniture, Sconces, branches, Braseras etc they were all of massive silver, and without number...', *The Diary of John Evelyn*, ed E.S. de Beer, vol iv (1955), pp 74 and 343.

3 Philippa Glanville, 'Boughton Silver', in *Boughton House* ed Tessa Murdoch (1992), p 153, describing the inventory of 1709.

4 Their decline appears to be contemporaneous with the similar eclipse of large scale porcelain vessels. cf the memorandum of the East India Company directors to its agents in 1681 'in Chinawares ye are to observe that Beakers and Jars are much out of esteem, Basons of all sorts are in different request, but that which will turn us best to accompt are Cupps of all kinds, sizes and colours and all sorts of several figures and fashions, the more strange and novill the better'. Quoted by Robert J Charleston, 'Porcelain as room decoration in eighteenth century England', *The Magazine Antiques*, no 96 (1969), p 894. Despite this, in 1687 the Duke of Devonshire ordered ' a greate jarr, 2 flower potts, 4 little jarrs a bottle with a spoon' (Michael Clayton, *The Collector's Dictionary of the Silver and Gold of Great Britain and North America* (1985), p 196)

5 At least two Dutch garnitures of the 1670s at Welbeck provide useful parallels (E Alfred Jones, *Catalogue of the Plate belonging to His Grace the Duke of Portland KG... at Welbeck Abbey* (1935) pl XV.

6 Two unexamined and unexplained tall 'jars' at Knole are decorated with relief ornament in panels, perhaps in imitation of sawasa wares (copper and black lacquer) or carved lacquer. Whether they are Chinese, Persian, or Indian, or chinoiserie, and of 17th or 19th century origin remains to be seen.

7 Hackenbroch p.13 (who cites further examples)

8 Christie's, 24 November 1971 lot 63.

9 Maker's marks RC in a dotted circle and dating from 1685 and 1688, *The Age of Charles II*, exhibition catalogue, Royal Academy of Arts 1960-1 (115 and 118). Another pair of flat chased ginger jars apparently with en suite salvers, maker's mark D in script, date from 1682 (Sotheby's 21 June 1962, lot 15).

10 Only a few objects are known which fall outside these categories, including a unique communion cup and paten from Welsh Newton, Herefordshire, London, 1689, maker's mark IL, which is decorated with chinoiserie birds and plants. A rare flat-chased tea bowl with strutting exotic birds, maker's mark D in script, was sold from the Poor Collection, Sotheby's New York, 26 October 2005 lot 99.

11 Punch was a drink derived from oriental recipes.

12 Philippa Glanville, 'English 17th Century Chinoiserie Silver', in *The Jaime Ortiz-Patino Collection*, sale catalogue, Sotheby's New York 21 May 1992, unpaginated.

Fig 3.12 Candlesticks, silver, from a set of six, four with maker's mark for John Crouch, London, 1812, two with maker's mark for Edward Farrell, London, 1816. The Burghley House Collection

13 There was evidently a revival of interest in this form of decoration at the end of the 19th century, when Crichton Brothers and others produced high quality reproduction toilet services. There are many examples of plain silver vessels of the 1680s being 'improved' in the early to mid 20th century with flat chased ornament.

14 See David Mitchell, 'Dressing Plate by the 'unknown' London silversmith WF', *Burlington Magazine*, vol cxxxv (June 1993), pp 386 – 400.

15 Including the Sizergh Castle toilet service at the Victoria & Albert Museum, the only complete chinoiserie toilet service of this style in a public museum in Britain.

16 There appear to be no Huguenot goldsmiths in London who permitted this style to be used on their work.

17 Most recent writers now dissent from Carl Christian Dauterman's suggestion (in his seminal essay 'Dream-Pictures of Cathay: Chinoiserie on Restoration Silver', in *Bulletin of the Metropolitan Museum of Art* (Summer 1964)), that they are the products of a single craftsman or workshop.

18 Maker's mark for John Duck, Sotheby's New York 21 May 1992 lot 143.

19 See discussion in Sotheby's catalogue 14 March 1996 lot 170.

20 See discussion in Christie's catalogue 14 November 1998 lot 121.

21 'Upon his head he has a Cap, which on both sides has long Feathers to defend him against the Sun and Rain: In his left hand he carreis a Bell upon which he continually strikes till something is given him or you are gone out of sight. They seldome go about Begging, but sit upon the ground … with their Legs across like unto Taylors…' Johan Nieuhof, *An Embassy from the East India Company of the United Provinces to the Grand Tartar Cham…*(1669 edition) p 220

22 For the Beauvais tapestry manufactory. Original designs at the Musee des Beaux-Arts, Besançon, exhibited *Pagodes et Dragons*, Musée Cernuschi, Paris (2007) (Cat 3). An Aubusson example is in the Musee Nissim de Cammondo (no 330).

23 This suggestion was first made by Glanville op. cit

24 Gordon and Philippa Glanville, 'The Art Market and Merchant Patronage in London 1680 to 1720', in *City Merchants and the Arts*, ed Mireille Gallinou (2004) pp 11-24

25 Mitchell op.cit. p.400. On the other hand these may have been plaster or base metal patterns for castings.

26 See Dauterman ibid pp 17 -19

27 H A Crosby Forbes, 'Chinese Export Silver for the British Market, 1660-1780', in *Transactions of the Oriental Ceramic Society*, Vol 63 (1998-9), pp 1-18, passim

28 See Greg Irvine, 'East Asian Metalwork for the Export Market', in *Encounters; the Meeting of Asia and Europe 1500-1800*, exhibition catalogue edited by Anna Jackson and Amin Jaffer (Victoria & Albert Museum 2004) pp 232-3.

29 See Catherine the Great's assemblage in Maria Menshikova, 'Oriental Rooms and Catherine's Chinese Collections' in *Treasures of Catherine the Great* exhibition catalogue, Hermitage Rooms, Somerset House 2001, pp 202-237

30 Robin Butler, *The Albert Collection* (2006), pp 18, 318-320

31 J F Hayward, 'A William and Mary Pattern Book for Silversmiths', *Proc Society of Silver Collectors*, vol II, no 1, (1977), cited by Philippa Glanville, 'Chinese Influences on English Silver 1550 – 1720', in *Handbook to the International Silver and Jewellery Fair* (1987), pp 15 – 22.

32 Maker's mark of David Willaume 1705 Christie's 13 December 1967 lot 27; ditto 1708 Christie's Scone Palace sale 2007 (reported in *Antique Collecting* July/August 2007 p 21); ditto 1711 illustrated Philippa Glanville, *Silver in England* (1987) p 235.

33 Notably the early pages of Montanus's *Atlas* showing befeathered soldiers and archers. Nieuhof's *Embassy* continued to provide a direct source of inspiration on teapot decoration for silver and ceramics see infra; also Leslie B Grigsby 'Johan Nieuhoff's *Embassy*: an inspiration for relief decoration on English stoneware and earthenware', *The Magazine Antiques*, 143 (January 1993), pp 172-83; a white stoneware example c1740-50 advertised by A F Allbrook, *The Connoisseur Yearbook* 1956, p xii.

34 A flat chased chinoiserie basin by William Fowle, 1683, with ogival borders perhaps based on a Ding-ware prototype sold Christie's 12 June 2007 lot 102.

35 In all the published designs of the great Meissonier there appears to be only one drawing for chinoiserie design for an inkstand (Peter Fuhring, *Juste-Aurele Meissonier, Un génie du Rococo* (1999), p 285)

36 David Hume, *An Enquiry Concerning Human Understanding*, ed Eric Steinberg, (1993), pp 9-13, cited by Aldo Vitali, 'Retooling the rococo…', in 'Rococo Silver in England and its Colonies', *Silver Studies* (Journal of the Silver Society) no 20, (2006), p 73.

37 Christopher Hartop, *The Huguenot Legacy; English Silver 1680-1760 from the Alan and Simone Hartman Collection* (1996) pp 306-7

38 *Rococo Art and Design in Hogarth's England*, catalogue of exhibition at the Victoria & Albert Museum 1984, p 118.

39 Christopher Hartop, 'Patrons and Consumers; buying silver in eighteenth century London', in 'Rococo Silver in England and its Colonies', *Silver Studies*, op.cit., p 42.

40 See Peter Kaellgren, 'The tea-picker design on English rococo silver tea caddies', *The Magazine Antiques*, 1982, pp 484 - 489

41 See Hartop, Huguenot Legacy op cit, pp 320-323 and Ellenor M Alcorn, *English Silver in the Museum of Fine Arts Boston*, vol II, pp 166-167.

42 See Roland Michel, *Lajoue et l'Art Rocaille*, (1982), figs 238-241, and Desmond Fitzgerald, 'An Unpublished 'Chinoiserie' by Jacques de Lajoue (1686-1761)', *Connoisseur*, (1964), pp 109-113, 156-161.

43 See Richard Edgcumbe, *The Art of the Gold Chaser in Eighteenth Century London*, (2000), pp 45-48, 56-69; and Clifford ibid p 83.

44 However, the details on the Temple Newsam pot are taken from Pillement's *Etudes de differentes figures chinoises inventées et desinées par Jean Pillement* (nd), reprinted in *L'Oeuvre de Jean Pillement* ed A Guerinet, 1e série A – chinoiseries pl 66 and 69 (nd)

45 On the example illustrated it translates (left) chun and (right) fang meaning 'spring' or 'life' and 'square.

46 See Helen Clifford, *Silver in London: the Parker and Wakelin Partnership 1760-1774*, (2004), pp 65-66

47 Robert Clee, *A Book of Eighteen Leaves, Containing Diverse Subjects Calculated for the use of Goldsmiths, Chassers, Carvers, etc from Messrs Germain, Messonier, Sig. Cattarello etc*, 1737, See Clifford op cit passim

48 Notably a 26in diameter salver by George Methuen, 1753, weighing 259oz, sold Sotheby's 24 October 1968 lot 33. See also the trade card of Edward Dobson 'jeweller and working goldsmith' inscribed 'Brooks fecit' Sir Ambrose Heal, *Trade Cards of the London Goldsmiths* (David and Charles reprint nd) p 145.

49 Christie's 30 June 1965 lot 37, and Sotheby's 9 June 1994 lot 270.

50 See 1966 reprint by The Ceramic Book Company pl 195.

51 Sir Gilbert was also the owner of other fine French-inspired rococo silver, including a salver by Edward Wakelin, 1754, with an engraved cartouche closely derived from Lajoue (Rococo ibid p 120).

52 Accession no (64.315). See Hartop, *The Huguenot Legacy,* op.cit. pp 208

53 See Glanville, *Rococo,* op.cit. p 110, Hartop, op.cit., and Timothy Shroder's forthcoming catalogue of the silver in the Ashmolean Museum the drafts for which he has kindly shown me in advance of publication.

54 Clifford passim; Edith Gaines, 'Powell ? Potts ? Pitts ! – the TP epergnes', *The Magazine Antiques*, vol 87 (1965) pp 462-465, and ibid, 'More by – and about – Pitts of the epergnes', *The Magazine Antiques*, vol 91 (1967), pp 748-751.

55 Perhaps especially William Halfpenny's *Rural Architecture in the Chinese Taste* (1752)

56 Sir William Chambers, *Of the Art of Laying out Gardens among the Chinese* (1757), unpag.

57 Sir Crisp's sticks however relate more closely to a plate in Pierre-Edmé Babel's *New Book of Ornaments ... with trophies in ye Chinese way* (1752). See Geoffrey Beard, 'Babel's 'A New Book of Ornaments', 1752, *Furniture History*, vol XI (1966), pp 31-32, esp pl 65

58 See Timothy Schroder, 'The Duke of Sussex and his Collection', *Silver Society Journal*, vol 14 (2002), pp 40-47

59 Sotheby's 23 January 1964 lot 63. It is inscribed 'This font was taken from the cathedral Church at Lima', and has the armorials of Thomas Reynolds-Moreton, 4th Baron Ducie.

60 A hexagonal bowl by Paul Storr, 1812, sold Christie's 13 December 1967 lot 21; another hexagonal unmarked gilt teapot and an en suite milk jug, 1821, by J E Terrey sold Sotheby's 22 October 1970 lots 94 and 95; another gilt teapot, 1825, by Storr and Mortimer sold Sotheby's 10 October 1983 lot 523.

61 See Sotheby's 23 September 1982 lot 131, and 30 November 1967 lot 121.

Chinese Themes in 18th Century Gardens

'Mr Aislabie designs to erect a Chinese house of a pyramidal form, with a gallery encircling every story, upon the point of a ridge … One side is formed into a number of small terraces interspersed with rocks, which makes a Chinese landscape.' [1]

It may seem an eccentric gesture for a North Yorkshire squire to propose a 'Chinese house' on his rural estate in 1744. (The house was built, although not quite in accordance with Mr Aislabie's initial idea, on a steep bank at Studley Royal; it survived for 150 years). But in England – and only in England, it would seem – such projects were rapidly becoming fashionable features of gardens created in the new 'natural' and informal style. The landscape gardens created here in the years 1735-1765, with their emphasis on variety and surprise, presented a context in which small 'Chinese' structures, light and playful in design, could be introduced: pavilions, seats, bridges, and even 'Chinese junks' on freshly fashioned lakes.

These landscaped parks formed an appropriate setting for garden chinoiserie. For Chinese notions of gardening had often been invoked by those writers who, in the late 17th and early 18th centuries, suggested that the traditions of uniform planting and symmetrical layouts should be replaced by a more informal approach to garden design. In a celebrated essay of 1685 Sir William Temple poured scorn on the practice of planting 'Walks of Trees in strait Lines'. The Chinese, he had heard, created beautiful effects with 'Forms wholly irregular'. Joseph Addison, writing in *The Spectator* in 1712, praised the Chinese as respecters of natural scenery, while their English counterparts preferred to force plants into regimented rows and bushes into unnatural shapes. Accounts (and even engraved images) of imperial gardens in China were sent back to Europe by the Roman Catholic missionaries in residence at the court of the Qing emperors. Most lyrical of all was the *Particular Account of the Emperor of China's Gardens near Pekin* (1749) written by the Jesuit priest (and portrait painter) Jean-Denis Attiret. Attiret wrote of the 'beautiful disorder' of Yuanmingyuan, in which clear streams followed an apparently natural course between rustic stones and flowery banks; circuitous paths wound among hills sprinkled with trees, and in the valleys lay innumerable lakeside pleasure-houses of varied architecture, bright in their gilded woodwork and varnished tiles of many colours.[2]

'Odd & Pretty enough…'

Fig 4.2 Chinese House at Stowe, Buckinghamshire (detail)

Perhaps the earliest 'Chinese house' to be built in Britain was at Stowe, in Buckinghamshire. It was noted by a visitor in 1738: in the middle of a pond

Fig 4.1 *Chinese House at Stowe, Buckinghamshire*, engraving by B Seeley, 1750

Fig 4.2 Chinese House at Stowe, Buckinghamshire

stood 'a house built on piles, after the manner of the Chinese, odd & Pretty enough…'. The exterior was decorated with paintings by the decorative artist Francisco Sleter; within a japanned interior lay 'a Chinese lady as if asleep', and in the pond were models of Chinese birds 'which move with the wind as if living'.

After Lord Cobham's death in 1749 the Chinese house was removed from its pond at Stowe, but not demolished; it reappeared on his nephew's estate at Wotton in Oxfordshire. Here it remained, with one move within the grounds, until 1950, when it was brought to Harristown House, County Kildare, by the former owners of Wotton. In 1974 it was moved again to higher ground at Harristown. Finally it was re-erected in 1998 at Stowe (fig 4.1, 4.2).

It must have been a struggle to preserve such a fragile building through winters of frost and rain. As early as 1742 we learn that the Stowe pavilion was 'covered with sail cloth to preserve the lustre of the paintings'; nevertheless its external decorations must have been repainted on numerous occasions, and the most recent restoration is based on (at best) a 19th century version.[3] At Wotton the pavilion had the windows on its longer sides redesigned, and lost its footings, being located on an island hillock. Yet the building has survived through two and a half centuries of changing taste, moved five times, the last time in pieces – to be reinstated at Stowe. It now stands in a meadow, freshly repainted, a prodigal welcomed home, but lacking some of the accoutrements which lent it glamour in the 1730s – the reflecting pool, the platform raising it above the water, the connecting bridge with flower vases, and the glittering lacquerwork. The recumbent Chinese lady – a wax figure perhaps? - has also departed long since.

Another early pavilion, possibly even preceding Stowe's, was built at Woburn in Bedfordshire: an estate map dated 1738 is marked 'Drakly [Drakeloe] Pond wth. a Chinese Building on ye Island'.[4] It was designed, or at any rate executed, by the cabinet-maker William Linnell who, with his son John, was later to create the celebrated Chinese Bedroom at Badminton House. The Woburn pavilion must have been a spectacular little building in its heyday, as William Linnell's invoices for its decoration in 1749 suggest: it contained stretched 'cloaths' painted with 'Chinese orniments', carved and gilded work on the cornices and ceiling, a gilt 'copper vase' with green-painted leaves, and 'two dragons to the hand rayls'; the curtains were 'red check', and at the mahogany table were six painted 'India chairs'. Intriguingly, the inventory of William Linnell's stock taken at his death in 1763 included 'a japanned [sic] model of a Chinese summer house'.[5]

The island pavilion is gone, although subsequent garden chinoiserie is still in evidence at Woburn - the Chinese dairy (1789), the maze pavilion hung with glass bells (1833) and the 20th century Flying Duchess restaurant. Another survivor is the Chinese pavilion or 'India House' at Boughton House, Northamptonshire (fig 4.3) which was cunningly designed to be taken apart

Fig 4.3 The Chinese Pavilion at Boughton House, Northamptonshire

Fig 4.4 *Portrait of Richard Bateman* by Tournières le Vrac. Birmingham Museums & Art Gallery

and stored indoors for the winter. It has interlocking floor segments, 12 upswept roof panels, and removable side panels made of Smith & Baber's painted oilcloth. The Montagu family accounts show that the pavilion was commissioned by the 2nd Duke in 1745 from 'Samuel Smith, Tentmaker' and painted by one Oliver Hill. The next year it was placed 'upon the Terras' at Montagu House, Whitehall, overlooking the Thames. Estate accounts of the early 19th century document its regular maintenance and removals to the stables for the winter months. The Chinese pavilion remained here, through rebuildings of the house and rearrangements of the gardens, until 1917, when the pavilion was moved to the family house at Boughton.

Of all the early enthusiasts for the Chinese style, one deserves special mention: the Hon. Richard Bateman of Old Windsor in Berkshire. Bateman created a 'Chinese farmhouse', at some point before 1741, with a summer breakfast room downstairs and a library and museum above; the house had a Chinese porch, Chinese window ornaments and an outer gateway with three tall Chinese-gothic finials. A visitor in 1754 noted in addition 'a Chinese alcove seat, near which there is a Chinese covered bridge to an island'. Not content with these, he had himself portrayed (in 1741) wearing exotic robes, with a scroll inscribed with 'Chinese' characters, and behind him the vividly coloured Chinese porch of his farmhouse (fig 4.4, cat F5). In the 1750s he remodelled his chinoiserie buildings in a gothic manner, under the influence of Horace Walpole; Walpole was proud, he wrote, of

'having converted Dicky Bateman from a Chinese to a Goth. Though he was the founder of the Sharawadgi taste in England, I preached so effectively that his every pagoda took the veil'. [6]

The Mandarin Yacht

Islands were favourite locations for Chinese pavilions. In the royal park at Windsor the Duke of Cumberland, second son of George II, had a Chinese House built on an island in Virginia Water, the large artificial lake dug out by his veteran troops. In this lake lay China Island, on which a Chinese house was built in 1759. It consisted of three interconnected octagons, all painted in trellis patterns. It was large enough to sleep in, as an observer wrote in 1766:

'The outside ... is white tiles set in red lead, decorated with bells and Chinese ornaments. You approach the building by a Chinese bridge, and in a very hot day, as that was, the whole look'd cool and pleasing. The inside consists of two state rooms, a drawing-room and bed chamber, in miniature each but corresponds with the outside appearance...' [7]

The triple pavilion survived for over a century, occupied by gamekeepers in its latter years. For a shorter period Virginia Water boasted an even more spectacular piece of chinoiserie: the Chinese Yacht (fig 4.5, cat F10). The boat's history is well recorded, by the watercolour artist Paul Sandby among

Fig 4.5 *A View of the Mandarine Yacht and Belvedere*, engraving by J Haynes, 1753. Royal Collection © 2008 Her Majesty Queen Elizabeth II

others. In 1749 the Duke, an enthusiastic collector of boats of all kinds, had four vessels dragged overland from the Thames to the lake two miles away. The largest of these was a 40-foot hulk, which was transformed four years later by the Duke's craftsmen: the result was 'the Mandarin Yacht', expensively furnished with carving, gilding, and japanning. A long dragon was painted along the hull, its barbed tail beneath the stern deck and its long tongue extending to the bows. On the deck was placed a 'grand room', with striped roof sweeping up to arching dolphins and a tall bell-hung finial, with a grasshopper transfixed at the top. Below the grasshopper, and also on the short mast at the prow, were double-crescent motifs which were evidently borrowed from the outsize tradesmen's signs illustrated in Johan Nieuhof's account of the Dutch embassy to China a century before.[8]

Chinese and Gothic

In the 1750s the 'Chinese style' reached a wider audience through the rococo chinoiserie of the two great London pleasure gardens, Vauxhall and Ranelagh.

Ranelagh had a Chinese pavilion with a zigzag walkway over a canal; Vauxhall's dining alcoves, containing 'supper boxes', were described either as 'Chinese' or as 'gothic'. It was not uncommon for the two modes to be confused, since at this time few people had more than a hazy notion of either. Many improbable 'Chinese' designs for lodges and pavilions, railings and bridges were published in pattern-books, with upswept roofs decked out with cusps, finials and sometimes dragons. An ironic commentary on this confusion appeared in a weekly periodical of 1754:

'It has not escaped your notice how much of late we are improved in architecture; not merely by the adoption of what we call Chinese, nor by the restoration of what we call Gothic; but by a happy mixture of both. From Hyde Park to Shoreditch scarce a chandler's shop or an oyster stall but has embellishments of this kind.' [9]

Soon afterwards it was claimed that 'almost everywhere, all is Chinese or Gothic', and that the love of Chinese architecture in particular had become excessive – so that, if a foxhunter were to break a leg jumping a gate, he would be sorry if this gate were not 'made in the eastern taste of little bits of wood standing in all directions'.[10] The very remoteness and strangeness of China was of course a strong element in the appeal of Chinese and imitation-Chinese objects, but it also made them an easy target for opponents. Even now the term 'chinoiserie' can be regarded as one of several mildly xenophobic expressions, along the lines of 'Spanish practices', 'Dutch courage' and *'vice anglaise'*, which carry pejorative overtones in certain contexts; to this day the phrase *'chinoiseries administratives'* is a French equivalent of 'pointless bureaucracy' or 'red tape'.

'A true picture of the architecture of that nation'

In a few cases these structures were based upon specific Chinese prototypes, or were at least claimed to be so by their designers. In 1744 Admiral George Anson returned from three years at sea, in the course of which he had captured a Spanish galleon laden with treasure; he had brought his prize up the Pearl River to Canton, in south China, and spent several months there negotiating for provisions and repairs to his ships. After his return he helped to embellish his brother's estate of Shugborough, and one of the first of the new garden buildings was the Chinese House which still stands in its grounds. This was said to be 'a true picture of the architecture of that nation, taken in the country by the skilful pencil of Sir Percy Brett; not a mongrel invention of British carpenters'.[11] An early design exists which may well be that drawing by Brett, who was Anson's First Lieutenant aboard his ship *Centurion*.

The Chinese House at Shugborough contained Imari vases, Cantonese reverse-glass paintings and a rococo plasterwork ceiling, all of which are now preserved in Shugborough Hall. Like its cousin at Stowe, it was decorated outside as well as inside with Chinese themes. The Brett design shows trellis

Fig 4.6 Detail of Chinese house built on piles, from a lacquered screen. Pelham Gallery

patterns and a painted Chinese landscape of gardens and pavilions, and an early watercolour of the Chinese House (with the Chinese bridge, boathouse and boat) indicates outlines of green painted design.[12] In similar fashion the first of the several garden chinoiseries at Kew, dating from 1749, was a 'Chinesia Summer hous[e] painted in their stile & ornaments The Story of Confusius & his doctrines, etc.'.[13]

But for most 'Chinese' pavilions no particular Chinese precedent was deemed necessary. An upswept roof, bells or dragon finials, oriental scenes painted on the woodwork – all or any of these might be enough to win recognition as 'Chinese'. Some of the pavilions in English parks were no doubt inspired by scenes of Chinese pavilions depicted on lacquer or porcelain sent back from China. The pavilion at Stowe, which in its original incarnation stood on wooden piles in water, might have been inspired by a detail from a lacquered screen such as fig 4.6. The painted landscape on this screen in fact represents the waterfront at Canton (modern Guangzhou), which for nearly a century was the only place of trade available to European merchants in China. They lodged in 'Factories' (trading headquarters) which were spacious Chinese houses built on piles driven into the ground beneath the water. (It was not until the second half of the 18th century that the 'Factories' at Canton were rebuilt in a Western style.) It would be entirely appropriate if the Chinese pavilion at Stowe, a stylistic pioneer, was inspired by one of these waterside buildings through which so many Chinese goods – silks, porcelains, lacquerwork, and above all tea – made their way to the West.

The Great Pagoda

The most celebrated building in China, so far as 18th century Europeans were concerned, was the so-called Porcelain Pagoda built at Nanjing, capital of the early Ming emperors. Since the illustrations published in 1655 of the Dutch embassy to China, this imposing tower had been well known to readers of travel literature. In 1670 the Porcelain Pagoda was alluded to, if not quite emulated, by the palace known as the 'Trianon de Porcelaine' built for Louis XIV at Versailles. The Porcelain Pagoda was said to be the tallest in China, some 260 feet high, and nearly 100 feet in circumference at the base. The walls were faced with white ceramic bricks, and the roofs covered with green tiles highly glazed. According to a Chinese account, it was built in the 15th century to honour the Yongle Emperor's late mother:

'Its top was overlaid with yellow gold and with wind-and-rain protecting copper… From its lofty dragon-head were hung eight iron chains, on which were suspended 72 bells. On the eight corners from top to bottom were 80 more iron bells, making 152 in all. And on the outside of the nine stories were 128 lamps; below in the octagonal pavilion, and in the central pagoda, were 12 porcelain lamps … Upwards they illuminated the thirty-three heavens; and brought to light the good and evil among men, for ever banishing human evils.'

Fig 4.7 'The Porcelane Tower of Nan King', engraving from John Hamilton Moore, *A New and Complete Collection of Voyages and Travels*, 1778

Human evils were not banished entirely, however, for in 1842, after the signing of the 'Treaty of Nanking' (as Nanjing was then known) which concluded the first 'opium war', British troops 'went armed with chizzels and hammers, and brought away large masses of the porcelain'. A party of British officers climbed the pagoda to drink Queen Victoria's health in champagne.[15] Then in 1856 the pagoda was destroyed by a Taiping army, to prevent a rival army from using it as an artillery base.

It was surely this pagoda which William Chambers had in mind when he designed his dramatic pagoda for the Dowager Princess of Wales at Kew Gardens – a project far exceeding the 'Chinese houses' and pavilions which had hitherto been seen in England. As a young man Chambers had twice visited Canton as a supercargo with the Swedish East India Company; having turned to the profession of architecture, he exploited this early experience by publishing a handsome folio volume, *Designs of Chinese Buildings, Furniture, Dresses, Machines and Utensils*..., 1757. The designs displayed here, which were considerably more impressive than those offered in rival publications, were now regarded (not always deservedly) as the most authentic records of Chinese architecture available. They were consulted and imitated well into the 19th century; a close copy of Chambers's 'pagoda near Canton', as depicted in the *Designs of Chinese Buildings*..., was built in Philadelphia's 'Pagoda and Labyrinth Gardens' in 1829.

That however was a simpler, sharply tapering design of seven storeys only. The pagoda which was built to Chambers's specifications at Kew in 1761-2 is closer in form and detail to the Nanjing prototype, which neither he nor any other British traveller had visited. It is true that the Kew pagoda has ten storeys, whereas the Nanjing pagoda had nine – almost all pagodas in China have an odd number of storeys; the reason for this, presumably, is that Chambers followed the engraved view of the Nanjing pagoda published in Nieuhof's account of the Dutch embassy – or one of the many prints derived from it (fig 4.7, catF20) – in which an extra storey was mistakenly added.

Although 100 feet shorter than the Nanjing pagoda, the pagoda at Kew was the outstanding chinoiserie structure of 18th century Britain. Solidly built of hard bricks, it was also designed to astonish: in the architect's own words, its roofs were 'covered with plates of varnished Iron of different colours', and at the angles 80 large dragons 'covered with a kind of thin glass of various colours, which produces a most dazzling reflection; and the whole ornament at the top is double gilt'.[16] The roof-coverings and the dragons are long gone, but the building itself has remained through two and a half centuries of frosts, storms, and changes of taste. It was indeed, as Chambers called it, 'the Great Pagoda'.

This was not in fact the first pagoda to be erected in England; a six-stage wooden pagoda was built in 1752 at Shugborough, on a small island in the Sherbrook River, and even before that, in the late 1740s, a hybrid pagoda was depicted at Marybone House in Gloucester, with four roofs supported on a tall star-shaped base.[17] Studley Royal might have claimed an even earlier pagoda if William Aislabie had carried out his project of 1744 (as quoted above) for a Chinese building 'of a pyramidal form, with a gallery enclosing every storey'. But Chambers's pagoda at Kew was architecture of a different quality from any of these. Through engravings it became widely known across the Channel, and within a few decades half a dozen pagodas had been built along similar lines in the landscaped *jardins anglo-chinois* of mainland Europe.

Patrick Conner

1 Philip Yorke (2nd Earl of Hardwicke), 'Journal of What I Observed Most Remarkable in a Tour to the North', in J Godber, 'The Marchioness Grey of Wrest Park'. *Bedfordshire Historical Record Society* vol.47, 1968, p.132

2 *A Particular Account of the Emperor of China's Gardens near Pekin*, translated by 'Sir Harry Beaumont' [Joseph Spence], 1752, pp 7-45. For reviews of the 'Chinese' origins of landscape gardening in England see Sir N Pevsner and S Lang, 'A Note on Sharawaggi', reprinted in Sir N Pevsner, *Studies in Art, Architecture and Design*, 1968, vol.1, pp 103-7; and P Conner, 'China and the Landscape Garden: reports, engravings and misconceptions', *Art History* vol.2 no.4, Dec. 1979, pp 429-440.

3 See Emile de Bruijn, 'Found in Translation. The Chinese House at Stowe', *Apollo,* June 2007, pp 53-9

4 See Clive Aslet, 'Park and Garden Buildings at Woburn – II', *Country Life* 7 April 1983, pp 861-2. The inscribed map, by Thomas Brown, is in Bedfordshire and Luton Archives and Records Service (R1/237). The Woburn Abbey version of this map is without the inscription. My thanks are due to Chris Gravett, Curator of Woburn Abbey, for his help in regard to this pavilion.

5 See Helena Hayward and Pat Kirkham, *William and John Linnell, 18th century London Furniture Makers*, 1980, pp 146 and 173. The pavilion is noticed in Daniel Defoe's *Tour through Great Britain*. 6th ed., 1762: '…a Chinese building, where in summer, his Grace often dines with his company'.

6 Letter to the Earl of Strafford, 13 June 1781, The Yale Edition of Horace Walpole's Correspondence, ed. W S Lewis, 1937-74, vol. 35, p.359. For Bateman see John Harris, 'A Pioneer in gardening. Dickie Bateman re-assessed', *Apollo* vol.138 (ii), Oct. 1993, pp 227-223. The visitor of 1754 was Dr Richard Pococke: see his *Travels thro. England*, ed. J Cartwright, 1888-9, vol. 2, pp 64-5.

7 Passages from the *Diaries of Mrs Philip Lybbe Powys*, ed. E J Climenson, 1899, pp 114-15, entry for 16 August 1766. For this and all the garden chinoiserie at Windsor see Jane Roberts, *Royal Landscape*, 1997

8 Jan Nieuhof, *An Embassy from the East-India Company of the United Provinces to the Grand Tartar Cham Emperour of China*, tr. J Ogilby, 1669, p.81: 'A Street in Nanking'

9 *The World*, 14 February 1754

10 John Shebbeare, *Letters on the English Nation*, 1755, vol.II, letter 56, pp 261-2

11 Thomas Pennant, *The Journey from Chester to London*, Dublin, 1783, pp 70-71

12 See P Conner, *Oriental Architecture in the West*, 1979, pl.22 and col. pl.II

13 Walpole Society, Vertue VI, 1955, p.153; and see *Sir William Chambers, Architect to George III*, ed J Harris and M Snodin, Yale, 1996, p.55

14 *Chinese Repository* May 1844, p.262

15 ibid., p.264, and see Capt. Granville Loch, *The Closing Events of the Campaign in China*, 1843, p.184. The first Englishman to visit the pagoda was (or so he claimed) the 14 year old Harry Parkes, later to be an influential figure in Anglo-Chinese relations: see Stanley Lane-Poole, *The Life of Sir Harry Parkes*, 1894, vol.1, p.46

16 Sir William Chambers, *Plans, Elevations, Sections & Perspective Views of the Gardens & Buildings at Kew*, 1763, p.5

17 The Shugborough pagoda is illustrated in Conner, op. cit., col. pl.III; for the painting of Marybone, by Thomas Robins, see Arthur Hellyer, 'Only one of its kind', *Country Life* 15 June 1989, p.156.

Chinese Style in 19th Century Britain

Royal Chinoiserie

The extraordinary Royal Pavilion at Brighton springs from two separate traditions. One was the fashion, at its peak in the middle third of the 18th century, for Chinese pavilions and other garden buildings (see above). Of these the most spectacular, and one of the most durable, was the Great Pagoda at Kew, which the future George IV would have known well as a child.

The second tradition was a European one, and was largely the preserve of royalty. It was initiated by the short-lived Trianon de Porcelaine, an elaborate pavilion built for Louis XIV at Versailles in 1670, shortly after the first Dutch ambassadors to China had returned from their well-publicised audience with the emperor. The Trianon de Porcelaine's Chinese qualities were limited to an array of blue-and-white porcelain vases ranged along the balustrade at roof level. Nevertheless it was succeeded by several exotically-roofed palaces and pleasure-houses commissioned by members of the royal families of Europe. These were labelled 'Indian', 'Chinese' or 'Japanese', but bore little resemblance to any actual buildings in those lands.

More royal chinoiserie followed in the 18th century, including the circular Chinese teahouse at Frederick II's palace of Sanssouci in Potsdam; and 'Kina Slott', a Chinese-themed garden retreat built for Frederick's sister, Queen Lovisa Ulrika of Sweden, in the royal park at Drottningholm. In the early years of the 19th century King Ferdinand of Naples built a bizarrely exotic palace at Palermo in Sicily. Thus the Pavilion created for the Prince of Wales at Brighton may be seen as the last in a series of exotic pleasure houses which were commissioned by members of the royal families of Europe.

The revival of interest in Chinese style and decoration in Britain was largely due to one individual - George, Prince of Wales, later to be Prince Regent and then George IV. Before any exotic elements had been introduced into his Pavilion at Brighton the prince had demonstrated his enthusiasm for Chinese decoration: at Carlton House, his London residence, a Chinese Drawing Room was created in 1790.[1] Many of the decorative details in this room were derived from Sir William Chambers's design book of 1757. Already the prince was showing himself to be independent of contemporary fashion, since by 1790 the vogue for China had been in decline for at least 20 years. George may have been encouraged by the construction in 1789 of a Chinese dairy at Woburn, Bedfordshire, for the 5th Duke of Bedford; also indebted to Chambers in its details, the octagonal dairy by the lake was

Fig 5.3 Chinese interior from Sir William Chambers, *Designs of Chinese Buildings...*, 1757

Fi 5.1 James Gillray *'Reception of the Diplomatique and his suite at the court of Pekin'*, published September 1792. Royal Pavilion & Museums, Brighton & Hove

accompanied by a long covered walkway, a typically Chinese feature. Humphry Repton proposed further additions to the Chinese theme, which by 1833 was maintained also by the plants in the vicinity of the dairy, as the 6th Duke's head gardener observed:

'The Chinese Dairy is of octagonal form, and contains a great variety of valuable old China. The floor and slabs are of different varieties of marble. The windows are all beautifully painted with Chinese figures and various fancy birds; these, as well as the Portico, which surrounds three sides of the Dairy and Lantern, are also painted in the Chinese style, and the whole forms a very interesting feature in the Pleasure Ground. A small piece of water comes close to the base of the Portico, supplies the Dairy, and gives a highly picturesque effect to this part of the grounds. The banks, by the margins of the water, are planted with Acubus, Rhododendrons, Azalias, China Roses, Hydrangea, and other species that are natives of China, in order that they may correspond with the Chinese style of the building.' [2]

Fig 5.2 William Alexander, *Ping-tze Muen, one of the Western Gates of Peking*, 1799. Martyn Gregory Gallery

China Rediscovered

If the Carlton House Drawing-room and the Woburn Dairy reinvigorated the Chinese style, it was only within a restricted social circle. Soon after their creation, however, an expedition set out which, it was felt, might have more far-reaching consequences. This was the British embassy to China led by George, Earl Macartney. In his retinue, 95 strong, were two artists – the first professional artists from Britain to visit the hinterland of China. One was the Irish portrait painter Thomas Hickey, whose conversation was said to be clever, but his output negligible. The other was the young William Alexander, 'draughtsman' to the embassy.

The embassy's ships sailed up the China coast and landed as close as possible to Beijing. On 14 September 1793 the ambassador and his party were received by the Qianlong emperor in his summer palace of Jehol (modern Chengde). Many hoped that this event would induce the emperor to regard the British with greater favour, and facilitate trade between Britain and China; in this they were disappointed. The gifts brought by the embassy, with a view to impressing the emperor and his court with the ingenuity of British manufacturers, were accepted respectfully but without enthusiasm. 'We have never valued ingenious articles, neither do we have the slightest need of your country's manufactures' stated the emperor in a letter sent back to George III.[3] This response was foreseen in a remarkably astute caricature published in Britain a year before the audience took place (fig 5.1, cat F21): here the ambassador and his cowering retinue have spread our their tawdry offerings in front of a Chinese potentate reclining on an outsize cushion, who is evidently unimpressed; his only response is to blow a dense cloud of tobacco smoke towards the kneeling envoy.

But the embassy did result in a renewal of interest in China, which was fostered by a series of detailed pictures of Chinese locations, people,

Fig 5.4 Detail of Chinese 'export' painting, early 19th century. Martyn Gregory Gallery

activities and productions, drawn and painted by the diligent 'draughtsman', William Alexander. Three weeks after their audience with the emperor it became clear that the embassy was expected to leave. The members of the British party were allowed to make their way southward from Peking (now Beijing) by river and canal, and were thus the first British visitors to many places in China. (Western merchants trading to China were restricted to the port of Canton – modern Guangzhou – in south China.) Alexander's drawings were detailed and carefully drawn (fig 5.2); on certain occasions he was not permitted to accompany the ambassadors, but in these cases he was able to make use of sketches made by other members of the party. The resulting body of work was sufficient to illustrate several of the books which were published shortly after the return of the expedition, including the official 'Authentic Account' of the embassy compiled by Sir George Leonard Staunton, Macartney's second-in-command.

Chinese 'Export' Pictures

European artists were one source of Chinese designs; Chinese artists were another. For many years British merchants and ships' officers had brought back Chinese paintings from south China. These were paintings of a particular kind, known today as Chinese 'export' pictures, presented in a semi-Westernised style which was readily acceptable to Westerners. Often painted in meticulous detail, they were a valuable resource for European designers. The interior scenes in William Chambers's *Designs...* of 1757 (fig 5.3), which were utilised in the decoration in the Chinese Room at Carlton House and in numerous other chinoiserie projects, were evidently themselves derived from Chinese 'export' paintings (fig 5.4) rather than from any first-hand sketches of his own. (Chambers would have had very little access to Chinese dwellings, inside or out; the expatriate community was restricted to the precinct of their 'Factories', and as Chambers observed 'the populace are very troublesome to strangers, throwing stones, and offer other insults'.)[4] There can be little doubt that many of the illustrations in Chambers's *Designs...* were redrawn from 'export' pictures by Cantonese artists. So, too, were many of the plates in William Alexander's book *The Costume of China* (1805).

In January 1805 the Court of Directors of the East India Company wrote to their 'Factory' in Canton asking for 'drawings on Miscellaneous Subjects' to be sent back to their library in London; the company had already requested, and been sent, Chinese pictures of plants. Shortly after this some 350 Chinese 'export' paintings in gouache were duly delivered in London, and are now in the British Library. The pictures are in volumes devoted to specific themes - deities, boats, temple buildings, episodes from classical opera, gardens, furnishings. The latter include embroideries, weapons, trophies and lanterns.[5]

Fig 5.5 A C Pugin , *The Yellow Drawing Room, Royal Pavilion, Brighton*. Royal Pavilion & Museums, Brighton & Hove

The Pavilion at Brighton, and its successors

These drawings in the East India Company's library, and the many comparable pictures and albums brought back from Canton, were a rich source for decorators such as the Crace family. By the turn of the century John Crace had already been active in painting the interior of the Chinese Dairy at Woburn and at Carlton House in London. In 1802 the Craces began to decorate the interior of the Prince's Marine Pavilion at Brighton in a Chinese style: in addition to paintwork and gilding, this involved obtaining Chinese porcelain and bamboo furniture, and 'Japan' screens and cabinets – which might mean either lacquered furniture imported from China, or items 'japanned' in Europe in imitation of oriental lacquer.

The Craces' designs, in this and the following decade, brought a new dimension to 'Chinese style'. Making use of William Alexander's scenes, and Chinese 'export' pictures, they moved away from purely abstract themes and introduced a new repertoire of subjects, including mythical creatures and exotic figures from Chinese theatre and legend. The creation of an oriental palace at Brighton, inside and out, occupied two decades, with many changes in the process. As completed in 1822, the Royal Pavilion represented a major departure in the history of chinoiserie. Whereas mid 18th century houses might have a Chinese room upstairs or a Chinese pavilion in the grounds, China was now the dominant theme of the whole substantial building. In the new Music Room and the Banqueting Room especially, the sheer scale, the opulence of furnishings, the richness of colour, and the drama of plunging chandeliers and rearing dragons, evoke a 'China' of imperial extravagance and self-indulgence – something quite different from the gently whimsical realm of mid-Georgian rococo.

'Chinoiserie', in the sense of non-Chinese products evoking China, is a notion which, to a large extent, we have imposed on the 18th and early 19th centuries from a 20th century standpoint. For present-day curators, dealers and decorators it is no doubt important to distinguish clearly between Chinese objects on the one hand and Western objects inspired by China on the other. But in the Royal Pavilion, as in the 'Chinese rooms' of the 1750s, there seems to have been no desire to draw such a distinction. Chinese wallpaper, porcelain and hanging lanterns were accompanied by the work of British (and sometimes French) craftsmen. Chinese 'export' paintings were framed by dragons painted on the spot (fig 5.5, cat F30). Figures of Chinese dignitaries imported from China were supplemented by figures carved under the supervision of Crace and Sons. The theme of bamboo was maintained in much of the Pavilion: this involved bamboo furniture imported from Canton, but also English or French beech chairs simulating bamboo; and at each end of the corridor are cast-iron staircase balusters and handrails, shaped with knots and painted yellow-brown, which resemble bamboo so cunningly that even today we may be deceived.

Fig 5.6 William Daniell, *Fishing Temple, Virginia Water*. Royal Pavilion & Museums, Brighton & Hove

Numerous other 'Chinese' projects belong to the first three decades of the 19th century – several unexecuted designs by Humphry Repton, the pagoda fountain at Alton Towers (which is still in place), J B Papworth's design for Sparrow's Tea Warehouse in Ludgate Hill (cat F38), and the design by J T Serres for the façade of the Royal Coburg Theatre. Much the grandest was the sumptuous Fishing Temple created for George IV by Jeffry Wyatville and Frederick Crace on the banks of Virginia Water (fig 5.6, cat F39). This was a very elaborate building with three rooms and three pagoda-roofs, and a verandah running around it. Visiting the Fishing Temple in 1826, Lady Holland described it as

'...in the Chinese taste, full of gilt dragons for ornaments; rather too expensive, on dit, considering Windsor, Buckingham House, York House and the state of the country'.[6]

But the death of the king in 1830 also signalled the demise of Chinese *jeux d'esprit* in England. China was closely associated in the public mind with an unpopular and extravagant monarch, and perhaps with the frivolities of the Georgian era in general. In the succeeding years other styles found favour, above all the many varieties of gothic. In this new era a style required a rationale, a cultural context, to prevail. In the face of such earnest and eloquent advocates as John Ruskin, convinced that art sprang from the soul of a nation, Chinese fashion made little headway in Britain.

Fig 5.7 Pagoda entrance to the Chinese Collection, Hyde Park, 1844

Opium and Empire

Political circumstances also had a bearing on the matter. In 1834 the monopoly which had long been enjoyed by the East India Company in China came to an end; the 'free merchants' who continued to trade in Canton (modern Guangzhou) adopted a more belligerent attitude toward their hosts. The evangelical movement encouraged the notion that conflict between East and West was inevitable and, ultimately, to be welcomed. 'Better fifty years of Europe than a cycle of Cathay' declared the protagonist of *Locksley Hall* in 1835, and although he may not have spoken for the young Tennyson himself, he does seem to have represented the feelings of many who believed that Britain's wealth and empire were divinely ordained.

In south China itself, tensions became open hostilities after the Imperial Commissioner in 1839, Lin Zexu, charged with eradicating the illicit trade in opium, forced the British and American merchants to surrender their opium holdings – which were then dissolved in water and lime and flushed out into the Pearl River. The British merchants lobbied their allies in Parliament, and a retaliatory force was sent out to China; the result was the first 'opium war'.

Hostilities with China continued intermittently until 1860. Under these circumstances, and presented with anti-Chinese sentiments in the press, British observers found it difficult to regard Chinese civilisation in the sympathetic light which had prevailed in the 18th century. Free market capitalism and narrow-minded Protestantism formed an uneasy alliance in justifying British aggression. It was a Hong Kong-based Scottish missionary - later the first Professor of Chinese at Oxford – who claimed in 1853, after one period of conflict and shortly before another, that 'China was sure to go to pieces when it came into collision with a Christianly-civilised power'.[7]

By this time the topography and artefacts of China were more familiar in Britain than ever before. In 1838 a huge painting of Canton, with explanatory key and booklet, was shown at Robert Burford's popular Panorama in Leicester Square, London. After the Treaty of Nanking (Nanjing) was signed in August 1842, bringing the first Opium War to an end, the Panorama presented Burford's 'View of the city of Nanking, and the surrounding country'; this included a full account of the celebrated 'Porcelain Pagoda'.

At the same time the Chinese Collection was attracting large crowds in London. This exhibition of Chinese everyday objects and works of art had been assembled by the Philadelphia merchant Nathan Dunn, and brought over to London, where it opened in 1842 at St George's Place, Hyde Park Corner. It contained some 1,300 exhibits, accompanied by a detailed catalogue, which claimed that 'as a means of education, this Collection is invaluable ... Here we have an empire with all its varieties of light and shade, its experience, its mind, and the results of both, for four thousand years'.[8] The Chinese Collection displayed a greater variety of Chinese items than did the subsequent China Court in the Great Exhibition of 1851.

Victorian Pagodas

Despite the plethora of information about China available by the middle years of the 19th century, there was little enthusiasm for Chinese styles on the part of British architects and designers. Chinese architecture and design did not entirely disappear from Britain, however. In 1840 the Fishing Temple at Virginia Water was about to be demolished on grounds of taste and safety, but it was reprieved at the last moment, and only in 1867 was it replaced - by a Swiss chalet. Queen Victoria and Prince Albert seem to have had no personal animosity towards the Chinese style. When they gave up the Royal Pavilion at Brighton in favour of an Italianate villa at Osborne in the Isle of Wight, the Queen might have taken this opportunity to divest herself of her uncle's exotic furnishings. Instead she and the prince incorporated most of the Chinese elements from the Pavilion into Buckingham Palace, where many of them still remain; indeed, Albert overrode his architect's objections to re-using the Brighton furniture, although it is not clear whether he did so on grounds of taste or economy.[9]

A few Chinese projects were executed in the middle years of the century, usually for didactic purposes. One was a part of the Chinese Collection itself - the kiosk or pagoda (fig 5.7) which had been designed by the Scottish-born architect John Notman as the entrance to the exhibition. This two-storey building, 'based on a model of a summer house now in the collection', was offered for sale in 1847, and bought for the newly established Victoria Park in Hackney. It stood on Pagoda Island in the lake, connected to the shore by a 'Chinese Bridge' added by James Pennethorne, designer of the park. The pagoda was dismantled after damage in the Second World War, when the park was occupied by anti-aircraft guns and prisoners of war.[10]

At much the same time a three-storey pagoda was built for Cremorne gardens beside the Thames in Chelsea (fig 5.8), following in the tradition of the chinoiserie at Vauxhall and Ranelagh. Here the pagoda was the central feature of the pleasure gardens, brilliantly illuminated by gaslights in crystal globes. The lowest storey was much the broadest, accommodating (it was said) 3,000 dancers on the platform, while the orchestra played in the smaller storey above them.

The pagoda-cum-dancing pagoda at Cremorne was built in the increasingly fashionable material of cast iron. So too was the two-storey 'pagoda' now at Cliveden, Buckinghamshire, which was made for the 1867 Exposition Universelle in Paris, was moved to the Bagatelle in the Bois de Boulogne, and then to Cliveden in the 1890s. Cast iron was combined with pierced ceramic tiles from China in the magnificent aviary built for the Wyndham family at Dropmore, not far from Cliveden; plans are afoot for its restoration. And at Brighton the West Pier (1863-6), the cast-iron masterpiece of the great pier architect Eugenius Birch, boasted dragons and more generalised oriental motifs, which set the tone for many of the piers which succeeded it in the latter part of Queen Victoria's reign.

Fig 5.8 Phoebus Levin, *The Dancing Platform at Cremorne Gardens*. Museum of London

Perhaps the most appealing example of Victorian garden chinoiserie was – and has now been rebuilt - at Biddulph Grange in Staffordshire. Here the estate, developed for James Bateman in the 1850s, includes a concealed garden known as 'China', with a vividly painted temple, bridge, zigzag railings, grimacing lion, gilded ox, stone frog and Great Wall. Nearby were the Scottish Glen, the Italian garden and the Egyptian Court. James Bateman's enterprise at Biddulph has echoes of Kew Gardens as they appeared in the late 18th century, when classical and Chinese architecture was accompanied by an Alhambra and a 'Turkish mosque'; Biddulph offered, on a more intimate scale, a similar homage to diverse cultures remote in space and time.

The last third of the 19th century saw a renewed interest in the culture of the 'Far East'; but this tended to focus less upon China than on Japan, which seemed to offer a fresh source of designs and aesthetic principles. The prevailing attitude to China was expressed by the young Garnet Wolseley, who had returned to Britain after taking part in the Anglo-French campaign in China of 1860. Wolseley observed disparagingly that the Chinese grotto at Cremorne Gardens was 'a very fair specimen of what is esteemed in China as the acme of all that is beautiful'. Wolseley likened the 'diminutive representations of mountains and rustic scenery' at Cremorne to the imperial gardens of Yuanmingyuan, which the allied forces had recently burned and looted. Wolseley's comments on those once-celebrated gardens outside Beijing might be taken as reflecting a more general disillusion in regard to China, and 'Chinese taste', in Victorian Britain:

'When we first entered the gardens they reminded one of those magic grounds described in fairy tales; we marched from them upon the 19th October [1860], leaving them a dreary waste of ruined nothings.' [11]

Patrick Conner

1 Illustrated in Thomas Sheraton, *The Cabinet Maker and Upholsterer's Drawing Book*, 1793
2 James Forbes, *Hortus Woburnensis. A descriptive catalogue…*, 1833, p.235
3 Quoted in J L Cranmer-Byng (ed.), *An Embassy to China. Lord Macartney's Journal 1793-1794*, 1962, p.340
4 William Chambers, *Designs of Chinese Buildings…*, London, 1757
5 Listed in Mildred Archer, *Company Drawings in the India Office Library*, 1972, pp 253-62. Further sets, illustrating the stages in the manufacture of cast iron and three pigments, followed in c.1820.
6 Earl of Ilchester (ed.), *Elizabeth Lady Holland to her Son 1821-1845*, 1946, p.47
7 James Legge, *The Notions of the Chinese Concerning God and the Spirits*, Hong Kong, 1853, pp 58-9
8 William B. Langdon, *A Descriptive Catalogue of the Chinese Collection*, 1844, p.14
9 See Geoffrey de Bellaigue, 'Chinoiserie at Buckingham Palace', *Apollo* July 1975, pp 380-391
10 See Charles Poulsen, *Victoria Park, a Study in the History of East London*, 1976, pp 60-62
11 Lt.-Col. Garnet J Wolseley, *Narrative of the War with China in 1860*, 1862, pp 233, 280

What's in a Chinese Room? 20th Century Chinoiserie, Modernity and Femininity

The first three decades of the 20th century saw a rich resurgence of chinoiserie in popular and elite design in Europe and America. Flower and butterfly motifs, lacquered furniture, red tassels and key patterns emerged as colourful and exotic aspects of British modernity that, in many ways, took its inspiration directly from the Chinese styles of the 18th century. Chinese dragons danced across the cushions, curtains and wallpapers of British drawing rooms, and fashionable women sported Chinese coats and even Chinese hairstyles. But this was a strangely paradoxical trend, quite distinct from anything that had gone before.

Chineseness was associated with femininity and modernity. As Western culture experienced the social upheaval of World War I and the excitement of the Jazz Age which followed, chinoiserie was linked with wealthy stylish women, and with new locations of mass entertainment, such as cinemas. However, Chinese styles were also influential within the design movement of Modernism, where fashionable 'femininity' was eschewed in favour of a stripped-back 'masculine' look. Lastly, Chinese design was seen as a style legacy of the 18th century, so that 20th century chinoiserie was greatly nostalgic for the supposed grace and elegance of British 18th century aristocratic living. However, interest in Chinese things also preserved some powerfully exotic myths about China's past at a time when Chinese society was being transformed from a land of emperors and pagodas to a modern, westernised republic. The word 'chinoiserie' describes something which has been authored in the West but which represents China. The celebration of Chinese themes in 20th century British interiors, whether they used Chinese or non-Chinese made objects, were themselves a piece of chinoiserie that created potent fantasies of China past and present.

The Wickedness of the 1920s Chinese Room

The Orient tends to be used as a site of the irrational and of desire – an enigmatic place outside history and modernity which supplies a satisfying sensuality not found in industrialised Western society.[1] In fiction, women who possess oriental interiors are often seductive and act counter to the interests of 'civilised' society.[2] The fourth book in John Galsworthy's Forsyte Saga, *The White Monkey* (1924), presents the character of Fleur as uncompromisingly modern and extremely fashionable. Galsworthy gives us a description of her architect-designed Westminster home, featuring a Chinese drawing room in an intriguing combination of ancient and modern:

Fig 6.3 *Queen Mary's Chinese Chippendale Room*, oil painting by Richard Jack, 1927 Royal Collection © 2008 Her Majesty Queen Elizabeth II

'The room to the left of the front door, running the breadth of the house, was Chinese, with ivory panels, a copper floor, central heating, and cut-glass lustres. It contained four pictures – all Chinese – the only school in which her father had not yet dabbled. The fireplace, wide and open, had Chinese dogs with Chinese tiles for them to stand on. The silk was chiefly of jade-green. There were two wonderful old black tea-chests, picked up with Soames's money at Jobson's – not a bargain. There was no piano, partly because pianos were too uncompromisingly occidental, and partly because it would have taken up much room ... The light, admitted by windows at both ends, was unfortunately not Chinese.'[3]

In this room Fleur also used a chinoiserie footstool and a red lacquered tea table, and she used one of the lacquered chests to hide the telephone, in line with contemporary design advice to disguise the mechanical. During the early 1920s, department stores such as Liberty were selling box-shaped pouffes with sprung seats covered in a variety of chinoiserie damasks and brocades, that opened up to reveal a hidden storage compartment specifically for gramophone records.[4] Fleur also kept a Pekingese dog, a new, extremely fashionable and overtly Chinese pet, which was seen to 'round the room off' nicely.[5]

As a narrative device, the Chinese drawing room signals a domestic disturbance. Fleur has never loved her husband, and constantly teeters on the brink of an affair. By the next novel in the saga, Fleur has become an apparently dutiful young mother, and the Chinese room undergoes a similar transformation into a Louis Quinze room in gold and silver, complete with clavichord; the Pekingese dog is replaced by a Dandie Dinmont terrier.[6] Possession of a Chinese drawing room therefore calls into question a wife's ability to maintain a spiritually fulfilling and respectable family home.[7]

A decent and well-mannered home would certainly have been at odds with the self-indulgence associated with oriental things. Indeed, according to one home advice book, *Good Manners* (1924), a Chinese room gives 'an impression of wickedness'.[8] The 1920s American film star, Clara Bow, created a Chinese room that was a symbol of her own exciting immorality, with walls decorated in red, gold and black lacquer, red and gold oriental draperies, a large red and gold sofa, Chinese carpets, cabinets and lamps, and a lacquered Buddha on a carved stand. She excluded natural light, burned incense and referred to the room as 'a *loving* room, not a living room', encouraging her public to view her Chinese room as a den of iniquity, and constructing herself as a thoroughly liberated woman.[9]

Studies of fictional representations of late 19th and early 20th century Chinatowns in Britain and North America have demonstrated that the involvement of white women with Chinese men, and Chinese culture, was frequently the catalyst for the moralistic condemnation of Chinese practices that had hitherto been tolerated, such as illegal gambling.[10] Sax Rohmer's novels *The Yellow Claw* (1915) and *Dope* (1919) depicted the downfall of drug-addicted white women in London's Chinatown at Limehouse, partly inspired

Fig 6.1. Evening pyjama outfit in blue silk satin embroidered with white dragons, c.1925. Royal Pavilion & Museums, Brighton & Hove

by the real-life scandal caused by the death of the actress Billie Carlton in 1918, in which Limehouse Chinese were implicated as drug suppliers.[11] *Dope* featured the Chinatown adventures of Rita Dresden, a drug-addicted actress, in the company of Molly Gretna, 'notorious society divorcée, foremost in the van of every craze, a past-mistress of the strangest vices' for whom the mere sight of Chinese people was 'deliciously sinful'.[12] Such negative reactions to fashionable women and Chinese things were widely found in the popular culture of the time, and perhaps it was precisely because of the subversive nature of Chinese things that chinoiserie successfully became a part of defiant modern femininities, focused on a new generation of increasingly independent women who smoked, wore make-up, bobbed their hair and sought access to higher education, professional training, and the vote.

The Book of the Home recommended a 'Chinese' room for expressing individuality, using a 'striking paper designed after the manner of red lacquer, or one bepatterned in oranges or adorned with birds of paradise … in panel form'.[13] Chinese dragon motifs were considered even more daring.[14] Drawing rooms were often considered as a 'becoming' and 'admirable background' for a hostess, so that interior decoration and dress fashions were interconnected.[15] Fashionable clothing was being sold within a 'lifestyle' package,[16] and so the daring dragons of the 'Chinese' room transferred easily to the latest pyjama lounging outfits, dresses, evening gowns and coats (fig 6.1).[17]

Chinese dress had had an influence on Western fashions from just after 1900, with the emergence of Chinese coat designs. The main characteristic of the Chinese coat was its wide sleeves and armholes, which were cut in one piece with the body of the garment. As well as Chinese evening coats, and even Chinese motor coats, Chinese tea gowns and dressing gowns appeared, and such designs were said to have a 'special smart "sackiness"' at a time when most fashions were closely tailored to fit the body, following the lines of a controlling corset. This new fashionable looseness may well have seemed very daring, especially as this Edwardian notion of 'smartness' also had definite sexual and sensational overtones, producing a garment with just the right amount of exotic naughtiness. Loose, unstructured oriental garments more famously came to the fore in Paul Poiret's Sack dress of 1911, and the more tubular dress styles of the 1920s continued this feeling of modernity through emancipation of the body. This even extended to the head in 1920, when a Chinese hairstyle became fashionable.

The Chinese hairstyle was perceived as a threat to the very livelihoods of hairdressers and hairpiece weavers, because it was flat and unadorned, the hair being pulled straight back from the face and then fixed simply in a low *chignon* using an ornate comb.[18] It was worn hatless and combined with pendant earrings, perhaps providing a useful transition between the high, full and elaborate styles of the pre-war era, and the simple bobs and close-fitting cloche hats of the mid 1920s. Using the terminology of warfare, hairdresser Emile Long described how 'this accursed Chinese mode … was to be the

Fig 6.2. Suggested use for 'Chinese Chippendale' pattern wallpaper, including an array of lacquered furniture. The Wallpaper Manufacturers Ltd, c.1920. Rare Books & Special Collections, Jubilee Library, Brighton

ruin of the profession in general and of hairdressers in particular.'[19] However, sensing that resistance would be futile, he advised all hairdressers to 'know the enemy' instead, and to offer the 'Chinese' style as a way to sell false hair and expensive carved combs. Such diatribes against the 'Chinese coiffure' paralleled 18th century anxieties over the infiltration of chinoiserie styles into Britain, but Long was also mobilising the more contemporary rhetoric of the Yellow Peril, a xenophobic European, North American and Australian response to fears over Chinese immigration.

Chinoiserie, Modernity and Modernism

Whilst the *japonaiserie* of the late 19th century called for subtle combinations of green and turquoise, dramatic colour combinations were an important factor in the vibrant modernity of 1920s chinoiserie. Late 1890s and early 1900s advice had been for plain walls – a reaction against the dark and florid Victorian interior – but by 1913, large Chinese patterns were being recommended, using rich colours on a black background for a modern impact. Black and scarlet were said 'naturally' to suggest a 'Chinese' room, clearly inspired by the colours of lacquer furniture, and a wallpaper became available which used the late 18th century chinoiserie willow pattern printed in black, scarlet and gold.[20] Red lacquer furniture was much preferred above blue lacquer or dark woods, although occasional tables in cream, yellow, and green lacquer were used as well, providing colourful and contrasting elements within these vivid schemes.[21]

A 1920s Chinese interior was also meant to be as glossy as possible. Architect Basil Ionides's design for a red hall or staircase recommended heavily-varnished panels of willow pattern wallpaper in black, gold and scarlet with black surrounds, with all woodwork also painted black and heavily varnished.[22] The floor was to be coloured scarlet, varnished and then waxed, and black lacquer-framed mirrors were to be used instead of pictures. Teamed with scarlet and gold curtains, scarlet upholstery with gold edges, cushions with large tassels and scarlet lacquer ornaments, this plan leaned heavily on Chinese influences to produce a very intense visual experience. Thus, a modern Chinese room was the very antithesis of dullness, and the gleaming copper floor and cut-glass lustres of Fleur's fictional drawing room begin to make sense.

Yet, Fleur's drawing room also contained a strange mixture of the overtly old and the avant garde – lacquer chests and copper flooring – referring to the earlier vogue for chinoiserie in Britain. Amidst a general revival of 18th century styles, the 'Chinese' designs of furniture makers such as Chippendale became fashionable because they seemed lighter and more refined than Victorian designs, making them seem modern even though they were reproductions (fig 6.2). Copies of older chinoiseries also presented an opportunity to exploit a nostalgia for the 18th century as an antidote to the bustling, brash Machine Age of cars, cinemas and department stores. A feeling of conservative modernity was created that upheld rather than

Fig 6. 4. Cabinet on stand by Ernest Gimson, c.1902. Victoria & Albert Museum

challenged the status quo for an upper class that had experienced a sharp decline in socio-economic power. Ionides designed a bathroom with Chinese wallpaper and a tasselled light fitting for Lady Diana Duff Cooper, and various other Chinese interiors.[23] Meanwhile, Queen Mary created her celebrated Chinese Chippendale room at Buckingham Palace, in which an old piece of chinoiserie silk provided the pattern for new wallpaper panels, curtains and upholstery (fig 6.3, cat F46).[24]

Such uses for chinoiserie were reassuring because they gave the comforting but misleading impression of unchanging societies in Britain and in China. In fact, following the mid 19th century wars that were fought over the right of the Western powers to trade in China, China's standing in the West had slipped from a seemingly invincible trading power to a society in decline with a vanquished, semi-colonial status. More armed conflict during the suppression of the Boxer Uprising in 1900 had further decreased its standing, and contributed to the demise of the Qing dynasty in 1911 and to the establishment of a new Republic. Thus, even as the mysterious world of emperors and mandarins was receding before the tide of westernisation, 20th century British chinoiserie maintained an illusion of those bygone pre-colonial relationships with China, and a more romantic, less troubling world.[25]

Conservative approaches to Chinese design also existed within the realms of British modernism. Designer Maurice S R Adams (d. 1941) advised readers to avoid both period reproductions and 'novelty' designs from the continent which he considered unbearably exotic, to the point of 'impudence'.[26] It was also his stated opinion that in the modern appropriation of Chinese lacquer, Chinese forms and motifs should not be used. Nevertheless, Adams's own work was inspired by the 'Chinese', combining modern versions of 18th century furniture and ceilings with black floors and mirrors, Chinese carpets, and black silk furniture upholstery decorated with gold Chinese dragons.[27] Adams's interiors were said to combine 'culture, mild luxury and good taste', treading a path between the traditional and the avant garde, and above all establishing that chinoiserie, far from being exotic, was somehow 'naturally' and tastefully British.[28]

Following the avant garde work of Eileen Gray and Jean Dunand in France, Adams, like many other designers of the period, was also creating modern furniture in art deco shapes, finished in a shiny coating of black lacquer (fig 6.4, cat C27). Even here, Chinese design could maintain its connections with femininity. In the mid 1920s, Betty Joel worked with female artist Cecil Leslie to produce modern lacquered furniture that was featured in an 'Ideal Boudoir' for the Daily Mail Ideal Home Exhibition as 'by a woman for a woman's use.'[29] However, reproductions of 18th century shapes still prevailed, with firms such as Hille producing lacquered furniture painted with Chinese figures and landscapes, whilst chinoiserie lacquered beds were sold by Heals alongside their more Modernist designs.[30]

Fig 6.5 Lampshade at Quex Museum, House and Gardens

Old chinoiseries also experienced a renaissance in the 'Chinese' electric lamp, created by using Chinese ceramic forms for the bases, and sometimes fanciful 'Chinese' shades as well. *The Book of the Home* tells us 'Lampshades of Chinese inspiration enjoy a perennial popularity, the more elaborate following the lines of the pagoda and Chinese temple, tassels and ornaments in the form of bells, and chains of beads festooned from angle to angle, forming the great feature to their decoration.' (fig 6.5)[31] Lighting effects were said to be particularly good when the base was made from Chinese porcelain or European chinoiserie ceramics such as vases, ginger jars and figurines, the latter being topped with a shade in a 'fantastic form such as a parasol or palanquin'.[32]

In vogue during the 1920s, the 'fantastic' nature of chinoiserie not only served as a location for European excess and social transgression during the 20th century, but also provided a reassuring set of continuities referring back to the 18th century. Chinese design in the houses of the rich was a nostalgic reminder of those former times when relationships with China were uncomplicated by warfare and immigration, and China appeared untouched by western influences. Conversely, the challenging nature of Chineseness, with its associations of threatening (and fascinating) exotic behaviour could be used to express some unsettling aspects of modernity because of a longstanding association with errant femininities, as well as providing colour combinations, fashionable shapes and motifs, and materials such as lacquer that were highly influential within avant garde design. Thus, chinoiserie was a fantasy of China that continued to serve the needs of western society.

Sarah Cheang

1 Suren Lalvani, 'Consuming the Exotic Other,' *Critical Studies in Mass Communications* 12 (1995) pp 263-86; Deborah Root, *Cannibal Culture: Art, Appropriation and the Commodification of Difference* (Boulder, CO: Westview, 1996); Rita Felski, *The Gender of Modernity* (Cambridge, MA: Harvard University Press, 1995) pp 136-141

2 William Leach, *Land of Desire: Merchants, Power and the Rise of a New American Culture* (New York: Vintage, 1993) p.106

3 John Galsworthy, *The White Monkey* (1924), rpt. in *A Modern Comedy* (London: Penguin, 1980) pp 24-5

4 *Liberty Yule-tide Gifts* (London, Liberty, 1922) p.35; *Liberty Yule-tide Gifts* 1923-1924 (London: Liberty, 1923) p.32

5 Galsworthy, *The White Monkey*, p. 41. Sarah Cheang, 'Women, Pets and Imperialism: The British Pekingese Dog and Nostalgia for Old China,' *Journal of British Studies* 45.2 (2006) pp 359-87

6 John Galsworthy, *The Silver Spoon* (1926) rpt. in *A Modern Comedy* (London: Penguin, 1980) pp. 293-299

7 Dudley Barker, *The Man of Principle: A View of John Galsworthy* (London: Heinemann, 1963) pp 205-206; James Gindin, *John Galsworthy's Life and Art: An Alien's Fortress* (Basingstoke: MacMillan,1987) p.501

8 Lady Kitty Vincent, *Good Manners* (London: Hodder, [1924]) p.63

9 David Stenn, 'Clara Bow: The "It" Girl's Notorious Home in Beverley Hills,' *Architectural Digest* (Apr. 1994) pp. 128-9, pp 268-9

10 Kay Anderson, 'Engendering Race Research: Unsettling the Self-Other Dichotomy,' in Nancy Duncan, ed., *Bodyspace: Destabilizing Geographies of Gender and Sexuality* (London: Routledge, 1996) pp 197-211; Marek Kohn, *Dope Girls: The Birth of the British Drug Underground* (London: Lawrence, 1992)

11 Sax Rohmer, *The Yellow Claw,* 1915 (London: Severn, 1975); Sax Rohmer, *Dope: A Story of Chinatown and the Drug Traffic*, 1919 (London: Cassell, 1929); Kohn pp 67-119. Mara L. Keire's study of the gendering of drug addiction finds that in America, cocaine addiction was seen as a feminine trait associated with prostitutes, effeminate men and the Chinatowns. Mara L. Keire, 'Dope Fiends and Degenerates: The Gendering of Addiction in the Early Twentieth Century,' *Journal of Social History,* Summer (1998) pp 809-822

12 Rohmer, *Dope* pp 86, 113

13 Davide C Minter, ed. *The Book of the Home: A Practical Guide for the Modern Household*, Vol. 1 (London: Gresham, 1927) pp 44-5

14 Mrs M Vince, *Decoration and Care of the Home: Some Practical Advice* (London: Collins, 1923) p.146

15 Edward W Gregory, *The Art and Craft of Home-Making: With an Appendix of 200 Household Recipes* (London: Murby, 1913) p.29; Basil Ionides, *Colour and Interior Decoration* (London: Country Life, 1926) p.73; Peter McNeil, 'Designing Women: Gender, Sexuality and the Interior Decorator, c.1890-1940,' *Art History* 17.4 (1995) pp 645-650

16 Nancy J Troy, *Couture Culture: A Study in Modern Art and Fashion* (Cambridge, MA: MIT, 2003) pp 44-7, 49-54, 66-7

17 See for example evening gown, Chimère, designed by Paquin with a dragon and clouds in a Chinese style (Victoria & Albert Museum T.50-1948), 1920s pyjamas with Chinese dragons (Brighton Museum C002882), and an evening coat owned by Anne Armstrong Jones, the daughter of Maud Messel, designed by Reville with dragon motifs c. 1923 (Brighton Museum C004021).

18 Steven Zdatny, ed. *Hairstyles and Fashion: A Hairdresser's History of Paris, 1910-1920* (Oxford: Oxford University Press) p.194

19 Emile Long quoted in Zdatny, ibid p.183-5

20 Ionides, op.cit. p.63

21 Ionides, op.cit. pp 40, 61; Minter p.43; R. Randal Phillips and Ellen Woolrich, Furnishing the Home (London: *Country Life*, 1921) p.132

22 Ionides, op.cit. p.59

23 Ionides, op.cit. p.22 facing, p.23 facing and p.68 facing

24 H Clifford Smith, *Buckingham Palace: Its Furniture Decoration and History* (London: *Country Life*, 1931) pp 71-9

25 Whilst only small portions of China were British colonies, such as the island of Hong Kong, China was a colonial interest within the British empire. Sino-British relationships in the late19th and early 20th centuries were formed in relation to a backdrop of imperialism, and China, its cultures and its peoples were subjected to Western colonial attitudes and interventions.

26 Maurice S R Adams, *Modern Decorative Art: A Series of Two Hundred Examples of Interior Decoration, Furniture, Lighting Fittings and Other Ornamental Features* (London: Batsford, 1930) pp 6-7

27 Ibid pp 59-62

28 *Daily Mail Ideal Home Exhibition*: Olympia: March 2nd-25th 1925 (London: Ideal Home Exhibition, 1925) pp 219, 220; Adams p.59

29 Ibid p.220

30 Susanna Goodden, *At the Sign of the Fourposter: A History of Heal's* (London: Heal and Son, 1984) p.43; Sutherland Lyall, *Hille: 75 Years of British Furniture* (London: Elron, 1981) pp 9, 73, 71

31 Minter, op. cit. p.80

32 Ibid pp 80-81

List of Works

The object list is correct at the time of going to press. Dimensions are in cm, height x width x depth. Unless specified, a single dimension indicates the height of the object.

F13 Paul Sandby and Thomas Sandby,
Virginia Water from the Manor Lodge, c.1754
Royal Collection © 2008 Her Majesty
Queen Elizabeth II

Silver and Metalwork

A1 Pair of salvers
Silver-gilt, with flat-chased chinoiseries
5.7 x 20.2cm
Unmarked, probably London, c.1682.
Others in the set with
maker's mark D

Part of a large (dispersed) toilet service. The chinoiseries are taken from travel books as well as porcelain and lacquer. The snuffers and tray from the Ashmolean Museum, Oxford, are probably by the same maker (cat A4).

Birmingham Museums & Art Gallery, 1968M3 1&2

A2 Box
Silver, cast and chased
7.4cm (width)
Maker's mark PD, probably
London, c.1670

The box carries an inscription indicating that it was given by King Charles II to his mistress, Nell Gwynne. The design resembles Chinese lacquer and is almost identical to a Chinese silver example of the same date.

Victoria & Albert Museum, M700-1926

Main image: A8 Tankard, 1685. The Rosalinde and Arthur Gilbert Collection on loan to the Victoria & Albert Museum

A3 Five piece garniture
Silver
46cm (max. ht.)
Unmarked, except two covered beakers,
London, 1676; the rest c.1670-1680

Garnitures of 'massy plate', imitating Chinese porcelain, were used as part of the furnishings of opulent bedrooms and dressing rooms during the Restoration period.

Private collection

A4 Snuffers and tray
Silver, chased with chinoiseries
22.9cm (length of tray)
Maker's mark D on tray; WB on Snuffers
London, 1682

Snuffers and trays, together with candlesticks, were often included as parts of toilet services. The centre of the tray is chased with a bird, a cat, and oriental figures, probably derived from Chinese or Japanese porcelain. The tray may well be by the same maker as the salvers from Birmingham (cat A1).

Ashmolean Museum, Oxford, WA2002.230.1&2

A4 Snuffers and tray

A5 Monteith
Silver, chased with chinoiseries
14.2 x 29cm
George Garthorne, London, 1684

This is one of the earliest known monteiths. The body is chased with figures which are comparable to those on the monteith from Erdigg (cat A11). No single source has been traced, but similar scenes are found on textiles, lacquer, porcelain and in travel books. Possibly named after William Graham, Earl of Monteith (c.1634-94), who wore the bottom of his cloak notched, Monteiths could be used as punch bowls, or for cooling glasses.

Ashmolean Museum, Oxford, WA2000.14

A5 Monteith

A6 Two-handled cup and cover
Silver, chased with chinoiseries
18.4cm
John Jackson I, London, 1684

The Holburne Museum of Art, Bath, S8

A6 Two-handled cup and cover

A7 Chocolate cup and cover

Gold, chased with chinoiseries
11.2cm
Ralph Leake, London, c.1685

The chinoiseries on this exceptionally rare piece derive from prints, printed textiles or imported porcelain. The cup itself imitates stonewares by the Elers brothers which in turn are based on redwares from Yixing, China. The cup was found in the 19th century in a pond at Knowsley, Lancashire, a seat of the Earls of Derby. It may have been made for Elizabeth, Countess of Derby, to whom Stalker and Parker's Treatise of Japaning and Varnishing (1688) was dedicated.

Leeds Museums & Galleries (Temple Newsam), 2002.0082

A7 Chocolate cup and cover

A8 Tankard

Silver, chased with chinoiseries
21.3cm
Maker's mark R, London, 1685
Engraved in the mid-18th century with the arms of Weekes of Hurstpierpoint.

The Rosalinde and Arthur Gilbert Collection on loan to the Victoria & Albert Museum, 1996/130

A8 Tankard

A9 Teapot

Silver-gilt
14.6cm
Maker's mark RH, probably London, c.1685

This is one of the earliest surviving teapots. Its shape is based on a Chinese porcelain wine pot.

Victoria & Albert Museum, M48-1939

A9 Teapot

A10 Cup, cover and stand

Silver, cast and chased
14.8cm
Unmarked, Chinese, late 17th century

The cup and cover are almost certainly Chinese, made for the export market. The decoration imitates Sawasa ware (a combination of copper and black lacquer) or carved lacquer. The handles are in the form of a sprig of fungus, a sign of longevity. The cup may have been acquired by King George IV in 1826, when there was renewed interest in genuine Chinese silver.

The Royal Collection, RCIN 50264

A10 Cup, cover and stand

A11 Monteith

Silver, chased with chinoiseries
33cm (diameter)
Maker's mark TA or IA in monogram, London, 1689

The sides are flat-chased with panels of fantastically clad Orientals and exotic plants. One of the figures, a Chinaman wearing a vast feathered hat, derives from an engraving of a mendicant in Nieuhof's Embassy. *See also cat A5.*

Erddig, The Yorke Collection (The National Trust)

A11 Monteith

A12 Tea kettle

Silver-gilt
19cm
Pierre Harache, London, 1695

The compressed hexagonal shape is derived from Chinese wine pots. The body has cast and chased scenes of 'India' figures riding and hunting.

The Burghley House Collection

A12 Tea kettle

A13 Tea bowl and saucer

Silver
5.4cm (bowl); 11.4cm (diam. of saucer)
Saucer with maker's mark of Mark Paillet, London, 1700

An extremely rare survival, the bowl or cup was highly impractical because the British, unlike the Chinese, preferred to take their tea hot. The fluting and scalloped borders imitate contemporary Chinese porcelain chrysanthemum dishes.

The Holburne Museum of Art, Bath, S442a 1-2

A13 Tea bowl and saucer

A14 Sauce boat

Silver, cast, chased and embossed
20.5cm; 22.7cm (length)
Indistinct marks. Probably London, c.1740-50
Attributed to James Shruder

A rare example of chinoiserie associated with the dining table rather than the service of tea. Chased with a rococo repertoire of scrolls and shells, the dragon handle could be read as either Chinese or gothic.

Ashmolean Museum, Oxford, WA1959.40.2.1

A14 Sauce boat

A15 Surtout de table (centrepiece)

Silver-gilt
44.5cm
Claude Ballin II, Paris, 1747

This extremely rare example of French chinoiserie silver, made by the French royal goldsmith, was probably ordered by Sir Gilbert Heathcote (1723-1785) of Normanton Park, Rutland direct from Paris. It is Ballin's finest surviving work in a fully-developed rococo style. The gilding is probably early 19th century.

Private collection

A15 Surtout de table (centrepiece)

A16 Tea canister

Silver-gilt, cast, chased and embossed
14cm
Paul de Lamerie, London, 1747

The rococo chinoiserie ornaments on the side panels include the 'cane cutter' motif. There are also cast tea plants and palm and nut trees. Chinese themes are particularly appropriate for tea implements; similar canisters had been made by de Lamerie since 1744. The gilding has been renewed.

Collection: The Worshipful Company of Goldsmiths

A16 Tea canister

A17 Teapot

Silver, partly gilt
16.8cm
Chinese, c.1680 with unmarked English handle and spout, c.1750

The teapot has been adapted from a Chinese hexagonal jar, possibly a tea canister.

Victoria & Albert Museum, M69-1955

A17 Teapot

A18 Ho ho bird

Silver, gold and diamonds
5.5cm (length)
Probably English, c.1750

The ho ho bird derives its curious name from the Japanese word for a phoenix. In Chinese mythology, it was a bird of good omen emblematic of the empress. This rare diamond example was intended as a hair ornament.

Wartski, London

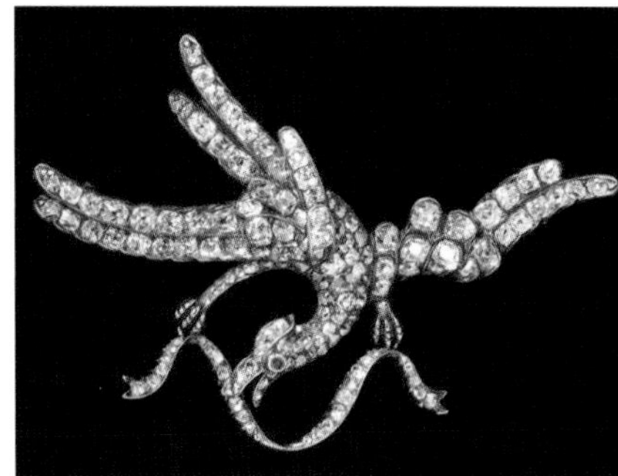

A18 Ho ho bird

A19 Three tea canisters

Silver, in a shagreen case
12.6cm (the larger); 12.3cm (the two smaller)
Two with maker's mark for Thomas Heming, London, 1751; the larger with maker's mark for Eliza Godfrey and rubbed date letter, c.1750; the case with maker's mark for James Waters

The canisters represent an interesting group belonging to the period 1745-1755 characterised by crowded and complex scenes possibly derived from the engraved designs of Jacques de Lajoue (1688-1761).

From a private collection

A20 Teapot

Silver
15cm
Maker's mark for Samuel Courtauld, London, 1748

Teapots in the rococo chinoiserie idiom are rare. This example has chased figurative scenes of Chinamen smoking and taking tea.

Private collection

A20 Teapot

A21 Tea urn

Silver, chased with chinoiserie scenes
46.6cm
Samuel Courtauld, London, 1760

Collection: The Worshipful Company of Goldsmiths

A21 Tea urn

A22 Flintlock double-barrelled sporting gun

Gold, silver, walnut, iron and steel
139cm (length)
William Bailes. Trigger guard and butt plate with maker's mark JA, London, 1764-5

The gun is rather poignantly decorated with chinoiseries, a style very rarely used by gun makers. The maker, William Bailes, worked in Bloomsbury from 1744-1766 and appears to have specialised in this form of decoration. The chinoiseries are close to a design by Jean Pillement in pl. 52 of The Ladies Amusement *(c.1762).*

The Trustees of the Armouries, X11 4669

A23 Hot water jug

Silver, embossed with chinoiseries
26.1cm
Thomas Whipham and Charles Wright, London, 1766

The chinoiseries are reminiscent of Jean Pillement, several of whose books of engravings were published in London in 1755-60. Whipham and Wright specialised in tea wares in a chinoiserie style.

From a private collection

A24 Coffee pot

Silver, embossed and chased
34cm
Francis Crump, 1769

Two of the three figurative scenes derive from chinoiserie engravings after Jean Pillement (1728-1808).

Leeds Museums & Galleries (Temple Newsam), 1991.0008

A24 Coffee pot

A25 The Duke of Sussex's epergne

Silver
56cm
Thomas Pitts, London, 1761; some hanging baskets with maker's mark of Thomas Bumfriss and Orlando Jackson, c.1770.

The pagoda-canopied epergne (centrepiece) was one of the most delightful of all manifestations of rococo chinoiserie. The design probably relates to 'Chinese' garden pavilions by William Halfpenny and others. The epergne is engraved with the initial S below a royal ducal coronet for HRH Prince Augustus Frederick, Duke of Sussex (1773-1843).

Private collection

A25 The Duke of Sussex's epergne

A26 Tea canister

Silver-gilt, cast and engraved
10.8cm
Louisa Courtauld and
George Cowles, London, 1773

Engraved with Chinese characters for 'upper', 'spring' and 'direction'. The cube-shaped tea tub, imitating the chests in which tea was exported to Europe, were popular from the 1760s to the 1790s.

Victoria & Albert Museum, M28-1934

A26 Tea canister

A27 Tea canister

Silver, engraved with chinoiseries
10.8cm
Robert Makepeace and Richard Carter, London, 1788

The engraved scenes are taken directly from pl. 148 of The Ladies Amusement or, Whole Art of Japaning Made Easy, *published from 1758. Many of the designs are by Jean Pillement (1728-1808), who remained a popular source well into the Regency period.*

Private collection

A27 Tea canister

A28 Teapot and stand

Silver-gilt
14.8cm
Paul Storr, London, 1812

The teapot was probably designed by William Beckford (1760-1844) with his friend and collaborator Gregorio Franchi (1770-1828). It imitates Chinese porcelain and Indian hard stone vessels.

Courtesy of the Trustees of the National Museums Scotland

A28 Teapot and stand

A29 Bowl

Silver-gilt
6.2cm
James Aldridge, London, 1812

Probably designed by William Beckford and Gregorio Franchi (cat A28). The bowl imitates Qianlong porcelain or metalwork.

Victoria & Albert Museum, M289-1976

A29 Bowl

A30 Pair of candlesticks

Silver, cast and chased
30cm
John Crouch, London, 1812

From a set of six, two by Crouch and two by Edward Farrell, 1816. The candlesticks are copies of a pair by Phillips Garden, 1756, for Sir Crisp Gascoyne.

The Burghley House Collection

A30 Pair of candlesticks

A31 Pair of candlesticks

Silver, cast and chased
35.1cm
Edward Farrell, London, 1821

The candlesticks are similar to those from Burghley (cat. A30), which are copies of a 1756 prototype by Phillips Garden. The bases, however, take the form of rustic drinking figures reminiscent of the work of David Teniers II (1610-1690). This illustrates extreme Regency eclecticism and the way makers enjoyed augmenting 18th century prototypes. The candlesticks (from a set of four) are engraved with the arms of one of King George III's sons, possibly the Prince Regent or the Duke of York.

The Rosalinde and Arthur Gilbert Collection on loan to the Victoria & Albert Museum

A32 Tray

Japanned tinplate, decorated
with chinoiseries
77cm (length)
Probably West Midlands, c.1815-1835

Japanning, the imitation of eastern lacquer, was applied to metal in the form of black varnish, which was repeatedly heated and then decorated. The chinoiseries are reminiscent of late 17th and early 18th century japanned cabinets and some features are close to engravings in Stalker and Parker's Treatise of Japaning and Varnishing *(1688).*

Amgueddfa Cymru - National Museum Wales, NMWA 50187

A33 Lalique brooch

Silver and enamel
7cm (length)
French, signed Lalique, c.1900

The brooch, in René Lalique's Art Nouveau manner, typically combines motifs from nature with the traditional Chinese motif of the dragon and pearl. In Chinese mythology, the pearl was associated with wealth, good luck and prosperity and was guarded by a dragon.

Wartski, London

A34 Brooch

Platinum, encrusted with diamonds
5cm (length)
English or French, c.1930

The brooch takes the form of the top storey of a pagoda. It is very close to pl.V of William Chambers's Designs of Chinese Buildings (1757).

Wartski, London

A34 Brooch

A35 Rosewater dish

Silver-gilt
50cm (diam.)
Harold Stabler, London, 1933

Commissioned by the Goldsmiths' Company, designed and made by Stabler with B J Colson and W E King of Wakely and Wheeler. The angular die-stamped ornament in the Chinese manner was a speciality of Stabler.

Collection: The Worshipful Company of Goldsmiths

A35 Rosewater dish

Main image: A24 Coffee pot, Francis Crump 1769, Leeds Museums & Galleries (Temple Newsam)

Ceramics

DELFTWARE

B1 Charger

Tin-glazed earthenware, painted
under the glaze
5.7 x 30cm diam
London 1664

The charger is painted with a Chinese figure holding a vase with a flower, standing under an arch between two columns. The source has not been identified.

Birmingham Museums & Art Gallery, 1941M67

B2 Caudle pot

Tin-glazed earthenware,
painted underglaze
22.5 x 30cm
Bristol, Liverpool or Holland, c1680

The vessel is decorated with groups of Chinese scholars and warriors in a landscape setting. The scenes appear to be taken from original Chinese images.

Royal Pavilion & Museums, Brighton & Hove, DA329854

B2 Caudle Pot

B3 Loving cup and cover

Tin-glazed earthenware
15.25 x 20.5cm wide
London or Brislington, c1690

The round-bellied vessel is decorated in manganese and two tones of blue with Chinese figures, one with a fan, sitting in landscape settings.

Sampson & Horne Antiques, London

B4 Vase

Tin-glazed earthenware,
painted underglaze
26 x 9.8cm
Probably London c1730

Royal Pavilion & Museums, Brighton & Hove, DAH47.29(1)

B5 Flower brick

Tin-glazed earthenware,
painted underglaze
12.8 x 7cm
Probably London, c1740

Royal Pavilion & Museums, Brighton & Hove, DA325472

B6 Plate

Tin-glazed earthenware,
painted under the glaze
37cm diam
Bristol, c1740

This delftware plate is decorated with elongated chinoiserie figures of the lange Lyzen type, standing and sitting in gardens. They wear distinctive rust-red jackets and yellow robes, very similar to those worn by figures on the so-called 'Niglett' dish at Bristol Museum, attributed to the Bristol potters John and Hester Niglett and dated 1733.

Jonathan Horne

B7 Plate

Tin-glazed earthenware,
painted under and overglaze
22.8cm diam
Probably London, c1740

Royal Pavilion & Museums, Brighton & Hove, DA321937

B8 Plate

Tin-glazed earthenware,
painted underglaze
22.8cm
Probably Bristol, c1750

Royal Pavilion & Museums, Brighton & Hove, DA321936

B9 Plate

Tin-glazed earthenware,
painted under and overglaze
22.8cm diam
London or Bristol, c1760

Royal Pavilion & Museums, Brighton & Hove, DA321944

B10 Plate

Tin-glazed earthenware,
painted underglaze
22.4cm diam
Bristol or Liverpool, c1760

Royal Pavilion & Museums, Brighton & Hove, DAH38.36

Main image: B74 Jug, Worcester, c.1760
Worcester Porcelain Museum

B11 Tile
Tin-glazed earthenware
12.7 x 12.7cm
London or Liverpool, c1770

Brightly painted tile showing two fishermen in sampans, probably part of a much larger tile panel.

Jonathan Horne

B12 Tile
Tin-glazed earthenware, printed
12.6 x 12.6cm
Printed by Sadler and Green, Liverpool, c1770

This sophisticated design shows an elegant woman with a child at her feet, fishing with a suspended net. Behind them is a fantasy Chinese garden pavilion with a partial sunshade. The image is based on Jean Pillement's illustration for January in his Allégories des Douze Mois de L'Année *(1758).*

Jonathan Horne Antiques Ltd, London

STONEWARE

B13 Teapot
Red stoneware, with gilding
8.9 x 12.9cm
David and John Philip Elers, Bradwell Wood, Staffordshire 1690-98

The teapot imitates Chinese Yixing stoneware wine pots, produced in Jiangsu from around 1000AD and exported to Europe from the 17th century. These were imitated by John Dwight at his Fulham workshop. The Elers brothers (originally silversmiths from Holland) made similar red stonewares in Vauxhall and later in Bradwell Wood, near Newcastle-under-Lyme.

Victoria & Albert Museum, C.4&A-1932

B13 Teapot

B14 Mug and beaker
Red stoneware
Mug 11.8cm high, beaker 7.5cm high
Elers-type ware, London or Staffordshire, c1700

Both the globular mug, with an engine-turned cylindrical neck and the inverted bell-shaped beaker are applied with stamped prunus blossom. This decoration is more frequently found on blanc-de-chine porcelain but red stonewares were probably imitating Chinese Yixing wares, produced in Jiangsu from around 1000AD and exported to Europe from the 17th century.

Leeds Museums & Galleries (Temple Newsam), 20/70, 21/70

B14 Mug and beaker

B15 Teapot
White saltglazed stoneware
12 x 15.8cm
Staffordshire, c 1745

The body has six relief panels with subjects taken from Nieuhof's Embassy… *and Athanasius Kircher's* Antiquities of China *(1667), which was published as an appendix to in the English edition of 1669. 'The Young Vice Roy of Kanton' (p.43), 'The Old Vice Roy of Kanton' (p.45), 'Ambassadors of Lammas' (p.125), a large plant inscribed 'China Root' (p.245) and another inscribed 'Round Pepper' (p.260) are taken from Nieuhof. The standing figures, inscribed 'Grand Tartar Cham China' and 'Supreme Monarch' [of the China Tartarian Empire] are from Kircher (opposite p.69).*

Salisbury & South Wiltshire Museum

B16 Teapot
White saltglazed stoneware
12 x 15.8cm
Staffordshire, c 1745

The body has six relief panels with subjects taken from Nieuhof's Embassy… *in the English edition of 1669. 'The Young Vice Roy of Kanton' (p.43), 'The Old Vice Roy of Kanton' (p.45), 'Chinese Men' (p.209), 'Chinese Women' (p. 210) and 'Peasants of China' (p.211) on both sides of the spout.*

Royal Pavilion & Museums, Brighton & Hove, DA310134

B17 Tea canister
White saltglazed stoneware, relief moulded
10.5 x 7.3 x 4.6cm
Staffordshire, c1750

The canister has two images from Athanasius Kircher's Antiquities of China *(1667), which was published as an appendix to Nieuhof's* Embassy…*, in the English edition of 1669. One side shows a tea plant* *as a vigorous shrub, impressed 'CIA or TE herb…', while the reverse shows a tree entwined with a vine, entitled 'Herb Teng'. Both images appear on p.87 of Kircher's book, illustrating Chapter VI 'Of Strange or Foreign Plants in China'.*

The Trustees of the British Museum, 1919,0503.108

B18 Plate
White salt-glazed stoneware,
enamelled onglaze
23cm diam
Staffordshire, c1750

The plate is painted with a baluster-shaped vase of peonies on a small Chinese table. This central motif is flanked by Chinese Buddhist symbols, including two of the Eight Treasures; an element from a stone chime (employed in Confucian ceremonies) and a pair of rhinoceros horns, symbolising happiness. Beneath is a pair of peacock feathers. The potters would have noted these emblems on imported wares.

Jonathan Horne Antiques Ltd, London

B19 Punch bowl
White saltglazed stoneware,
enamelled over the glaze
13.8 x 31cm diameter
Staffordshire, c1755

The exterior of this large bowl is decorated with groups of figures, vases and flowering trees. Some of the figures appear to derive from the same source used by the decorator of a saltglazed jug on loan from Temple Newsam (see cat B22).

The Trustees of the British Museum, 1920,0318.7

B20 Coffee pot and cover
White saltglazed stoneware,
enamelled overglaze
20 x 12.2cm diameter
Staffordshire, 1755-60

The coffee pot is decorated in a pastel famille rose palette with Chinese garden scenes.

Leeds Museums & Galleries (Temple Newsam), 4.166/46

B20 Coffee pot and cover

B21 Butter dish stand
White salt glazed stoneware,
enamelled onglaze
13.2 x 16cm
Staffordshire, c1760

Royal Pavilion & Museums, Brighton & Hove

B22 Jug
White saltglazed stoneware,
enamelled overglaze
28 x 19cm diameter
Staffordshire or Yorkshire, c1765

The jug is painted in a bright, pastel palette with three Chinese garden scenes with figures and large vases. The male figure below the spout has a bare belly and holds a long, looping snake.

Leeds Museums & Galleries (Temple Newsam), 4.155/46

B22 Jug

EARTHENWARES

B23 Teapot
Lead glazed, slip cast red earthenware
12.75cm high
Staffordshire, c 1740

This teapot has six relief panels with subjects taken from Nieuhof's Embassy… *and Athanasius Kircher's* Antiquities of China *(1667), see cat B15. A boat and a pagoda are taken from a riverscape inscribed 'Nangan' and 'A Cinnamon Tree' are both from Nieuhof (pp 59 and 225). The remaining scenes are from Kircher; two seated figures, inscribed 'A King 'and 'A Quene' (opposite p.36), and two standing figures inscribed 'Grand Tartar Cham China' and 'Supreme Monarch' [of the China Tartarian Empire] (opposite p.69).*

Jonathan Horne Antiques Ltd, London

B24 Tea canister and cover
Lead glazed buff earthenware,
relief moulded
10 x 7cm (16.5cm with cover)
Staffordshire, c1754

The relief-moulded figures are taken from Edwards and Darly's New Book of Chinese Designs… *(1754). The woman with a child in a jar derives from plate 21 while the boy with a bird comes from plate 22. The Trustees of the British Museum, 1887,0307.H.16*

B25 Teapot

Lead glazed earthenware, oxide coloured
12.5 x 16.5cm
Possibly Greatbatch, Staffordshire, c1760

As on the tea canister (B24), the figures are taken from Edwards and Darly's New Book of Chinese Designs... *(1754).*

Royal Pavilion & Museums, Brighton & Hove, DA323092

B25 Teapot

B26 Teapot and cover

Lead-glazed earthenware, oxide coloured
21 x 14cm
Staffordshire, 1755-60

This teapot is decorated with relief-moulded panels of scenes from Edwards and Darly's New Book of Chinese Designs...*(1754), on a square tiled background derived from early 18th century Chinese Yixing stonewares. Two of the three designs (repeated on both sides) are taken from plate 21.*

Jonathan Horne Antiques Ltd, London

B27 Teapot and cover

Creamware, enamelled overglaze
20.5 x 13.5cm
Staffordshire, c1760

This teapot is decorated with relief-moulded panels of scenes from Edwards and Darly's New Book of Chinese Designs...*(1754).*

B27 Teapot and cover

The central design (repeated on both sides) is taken from plate 32. It omits the central group and shows a woman bending over a basket of fruit and a seated child. It is flanked by panels featuring a boy with a bird on a stick, taken from plate 22.

Private collection

B28 Teapot

Creamware, enamelled overglaze
12 x 15.8cm
Cockpit Hill, Yorkshire, c1770

This is brightly painted with figures in gardens. One side shows a woman with a small baby and two boys, all staring at a white rabbit or hare. The hare signifies longevity for the Chinese and is associated with the moon. Hares are believed to live for 1,000 years and turn white when they reach 500.

Private collection

B28 Teapot

B29 Teapot

Creamware, enamelled overglaze
15 x 21cm
Wedgwood, Etruria, Staffordshire, c1770

The teapot is decorated with large Chinese male figures with windblown hair, in an interior at a table set with drinking vessels and stools.

Private collection

B29 Teapot

B30 Teapot and cover and mug

Creamware, enamelled overglaze
Teapot 22 x 15cm;
Mug 15.5 x 14.5cm
Swinton Pottery, Yorkshire, c1775

The teapot and mug are decorated in red enamel with Chinese figures.

Private collection

B31 Two teapots with covers

Creamware, enamelled overglaze
One 18 x 27cm; the other 15.5 x 22cm
Staffordshire or South Yorkshire, c1775

Both teapots are brightly painted with figures in gardens.

Private collection

B31 Teapot with cover

B32 Teapot

Creamware, enamelled overglaze
15 x 20cm
Yorkshire, 1775-80

This teapot is uniquely decorated imitating the Chinese linglong style; only an English tea bowl and saucer are known with similar decoration.

Private collection

B32 Teapot

B33 Mug

Pearlware, painted underglaze
12 x 11.8cm
Yorkshire, 1778

The cylindrical mug with a fluted ribbon handle is decorated with a Chinese building, fence and a spherical rock formation in a landscape. It is inscribed beneath the handle for 'Sarah Middleton 1778'.

Private collection

B34 Serving dish

Creamware, painted underglaze
46 x 35cm
Bovey Tracey, Devonshire, c1780

This unusually large oval dish is painted with a tall single figure of the lange Lyzen type, carrying a parasol, in a garden landscape. This simple design also appears frequently on Staffordshire creamware and pearlware.

Private collection

B34 Serving dish

B35 Mug

Pearlware, printed and painted underglaze
12.5cm high
Possibly Leeds, Yorkshire, c1780

The mug is printed with a Chinese man and woman engaged in outdoor tea drinking beneath a willow.

Private collection

B36 Meat dish

Pearlware, printed in blue
45.9 x 34.6cm
Cambrian Pottery, Swansea, 1795-1810

This large dish is printed in blue with the Swansea version of the 'Willow Pattern', known as the 'Long Bridge'.

Lent by Amgueddfa Cymru – National Museum Wales, NMW A 30613

B35 Mug

B37 Dish

Pearlware, printed overglaze
19cm diameter
Factory unknown, Staffordshire, c1800

The dish features a stylised landscape design printed in blue with figures, including a boy riding an ox gesturing towards a pagoda. It has a diaper and butterfly border, probably inspired by Chinese textiles. In China the ox or buffalo is the emblem of spring, agriculture and physical strength and is revered for its contribution to ploughing and milling.

Private collection

B37 Dish

B38 Garniture of vases

Pearlware, enamelled and gilt
Each 20.8, 21.2, 18.8cm high
Cambrian Pottery, Swansea, decorated by Thomas Pardoe, 1800-05

The two vases are painted with a ground of scales outlined in blue and gold. Reserve panels, with scrolling foliate frames are painted with groups of brightly dressed figures with parasols conversing in gardens or on the verandas of ornate garden pavilions. The reserves on the reverse are painted enamelled plants in red and gold.

Lent by Amgueddfa Cymru – National Museum Wales, NMW A 31122-24

B38 Garniture of vases

B.39 Tobacco jar and cover

Earthenware, printed, enamelled and gilt
23.3cm high
Davenport factory, Staffordshire, c1850

Each side is printed and hand-coloured with Chinese figures of warriors, women and baskets of flowers. The warriors may derive from William Alexander's illustrations to his Costume of China (1805).

The Bowes Museum, Barnard Castle, Co. Durham, X.3835

PORCELAIN

B40 Tile

Ceramic, enamelled overglaze
23.5 x 15cm
China, Nanjing, 1412-30

The famous 'Porcelain Tower of Nanking' was noted by all the early visitors to China and was the Chinese building best known to Europeans. It was eventually destroyed in 1856. The tile gives an indication of how impressive and colourful it must have appeared.

Private collection

B40 Tile

B41 Wine ewer

Hard paste porcelain, painted underglaze
11.5 x 14cm
Ewer Chinese, 1426-35; mounts unmarked, c1650

The ewer is modelled as a mandarin duck and drake, the female's neck entwined with that of her mate. The later cover is linked to the handle with a chain. Vessels modelled as waterfowl that swim skilfully on water without being immersed, were supposed to warn tipplers not to drink to excess at official banquets. Most blue-decorated Chinese porcelain was originally intended for export to Persia and the Middle East. When pieces, such as this ewer, found their way to Europe they were highly prized. They were mounted in precious metals to protect and enhance their appearance, and displayed in special cabinets. Almost all examples mounted in this way date from before 1720.

The Burghley House Collection

B42 Bowl with silver-gilt mounts

Hard paste porcelain, painted underglaze
13.9 x 23.6cm
Bowl Chinese, 1522-66; mounts hallmarked in London 1599-1600

The silver side handles are modelled as mermen and the hinged supports as satyrs. See also cat B41.

Victoria & Albert Museum, M.945-1983

B43 Bowl with silver-gilt mounts

Hard paste porcelain, painted underglaze, with silver-gilt mounts
9cm high
Bowl Chinese, 1570-1620; mounts London c1640

The silver-gilt mount lines the interior of the bowl and outlines the painted reserves with pierced trellis-work. Five circular medallions hang from the rim. See also cat B41.

The Burghley House Collection

B44 Wine vessel or teapot

Hard paste porcelain, painted underglaze, with silver-gilt mounts
20.9cm x 18cm x 12.7cm
Vessel Chinese, 1640-50; mounts London, c1650

The pot is decorated in blue with groups of figures of scholars and children in a rocky landscape. See also cat B41.

The Burghley House Collection

B45 Bowl

Hard paste porcelain, painted under and overglaze and gilt
7 x 13cm diameter
China, c1710

The exterior of the shallow, fluted bowl is painted in underglaze blue and onglaze enamels and gilt with alternating patterned panels probably derived from textiles. See cat B46.

Private collection

B45 Bowl

B46 Dish

Soft paste porcelain, painted under and overglaze and gilt
18cm diameter
Bow factory, London, c1755

The Bow saucer is closely modelled on a Chinese prototype (similar to B45). In addition to the patterned panels based on textiles, two are decorated with Buddhist symbols and there is a central design of a Chinese woman sitting on a green rock, holding a fan.

Private collection

B46 Dish

B47 Teapot and cover

Hard paste porcelain, enamelled and gilt
12 x 16 x 9cm
China, decorated in London 1735-45

The teapot with its straight spout (a typically Chinese feature) was probably brought to Europe undecorated. It was decorated, in London or Staffordshire, with blue bands and sprays of flowers flanked by red pagodas and Chinese warriors probably taken from early travel books such as Nieuhof's Embassy....

From a private collection

B48 Two teapots and cover

Soft paste porcelain
One 19 x 16.5cm,
the other 17.5 x 16.5cm
Chelsea factory, London 1745-49

These extraordinarily rare teapots appear to be modelled on Budai, the Chinese god of prosperity and contentment. The figures grin broadly, showing their teeth, as they each grapple with creatures that act as spouts; a serpent and a parrot respectively. These capricious and provocative forms probably derived from French models made at St Cloud.

Private collection

B49 Sauceboat

Soft paste porcelain, painted underglaze
7 x 21cm
Bristol, 1749-50, (moulded 'Bristoll' in relief on base)

Royal Pavilion & Museums, Brighton & Hove, DA322786

B50 Inkpot

Soft paste porcelain, enamelled overglaze
5.3 x 8.8cm diameter
Bow factory, London, 1750

The top is inscribed 'Made at New Canton 1750'. Until 1756 the Bow factory in East London called itself 'New Canton', not only because of the oriental style of its products but also because the factory building itself was said to be modelled on a Cantonese original.

Salisbury & South Wiltshire Museum

B51 Inkpot

Soft paste porcelain, painted underglaze
5.3 x 8.8cm diam
Bow factory, London, 1752

Royal Pavilion & Museums, Brighton & Hove, DA328183

B51 Inkpot

B52 Vase and cover

Soft paste porcelain, enamel decorated
33 x 21cm
Bow factory, London, c1750

A blue phoenix with flame-like tail feathers dominates one side. The phoenix or fenghuang ('ho-o' in Japanese) symbolises good fortune.

Pallant House Gallery, Chichester (Geoffrey Freeman Collection of Bow Porcelain, 1999), no 9

B52 Vase and cover

B53 Mug

Soft paste porcelain, enamelled
over the glaze
14.7 x 15.5cm
Worcester, c1750

Although there are hints of the sensuality of the prints after chinoiseries by Boucher, the decorator was inspired to create a fresh, new interpretation of the available sources and no direct quotation can be identified.

The Trustees of the British Museum, 1938,0341.38

B54 Peach-shaped dish

Soft paste porcelain, enamelled
3 x 18 x 3cm
Chelsea factory, London, c1752-3

The peach is particularly appropriate for chinoiserie decoration as it symbolised springtime, marriage and longevity in Chinese iconography.

From a private collection

B55 Teapot and cover

Soft paste porcelain, printed
underglaze, enamelled overglaze
12.8cm high
Worcester, c1754

The design is a careful copy of the Chinese 'Red Bull' pattern from the reign of the Yongzheng emperor (1723-1735).

Worcester Porcelain Museum, no 713

B55 Teapot and cover

B56 Two-handled cup and saucer

Soft paste porcelain
7.8 x 13.4cm
Bow factory, London, c1752

The cup, with gnarled twig-like handles, and the saucer are applied with sprays of abundant moulded prunus blossom. They imitate Chinese wares made in uncoloured Dehua porcelain, known as blanc-de-chine, from China's Fujian Province.

Pallant House Gallery, Chichester (Geoffrey Freeman Collection of Bow Porcelain, 1999), no 40

B56 Two-handled cup and saucer

B57 Sugar bowl and cover

Soft paste porcelain
14 x 13cm
Bow factory, London, 1752-55

This imitates blanc-de-chine (see cat B56).

Pallant House Gallery, Chichester (Geoffrey Freeman Collection of Bow Porcelain, 1999), no 39

B58 Libation cup

Soft paste porcelain
6.3 x 9.6cm
Bow factory, London, c1755

The cup imitates jade cups used for Chinese religious ceremonies.

Pallant House Gallery, Chichester (Geoffrey Freeman Collection of Bow Porcelain, 1999), no 44

B59 Vase and cover

Soft paste porcelain
14.7 x 9.5cm
Bow factory, London, c1755

See cat B56.

Pallant House Gallery, Chichester (Geoffrey Freeman Collection of Bow Porcelain, 1999), no 47

B60 Vase

Soft paste porcelain,
enamelled overglaze
23cm high
Worcester, 1753-55

Worcester Porcelain Museum, no 40

B60 Vase

B61 Mug

Soft paste porcelain, transfer-printed over the glaze
12cm high
Worcester, c1755

The mug is decorated with designs adapted, probably by Robert Hancock, from engravings by Pierre Aveline after a set of The Four Elements by François Boucher. Aileen Dawson suggests this may be the earliest use of French subjects on English porcelain. They also proved very popular and were used on Bow and Bristol porcelain. 'La Terre' (Earth), is set in a Chinese garden where a man kneels to present a pot plant to a young woman who leans languidly against a giant flowerpot. 'Le Feu' (Fire), bathed in clouds of steam, shows a seated archer being served a large bowl of tea at a wayside tea stall. Interestingly, the engraver has replaced the grinning pagod, who sits cross-legged on the shelf above the stall in Boucher's original red chalk drawing (Metropolitan Museum, New York (1984.51.1) with an angular vase. The 'Le Feu' composition was also realised as a porcelain figure group, known as 'The Tea-seller'.

The Trustees of the British Museum, 1971,0604.1

B62 Teapot

Soft paste porcelain, enamelled overglaze
15.5 x 22cm
Liverpool, 1755-60

The body is enamelled with a design known as the 'Beckoning Chinaman' (also used at Worcester).

Royal Pavilion & Museums, Brighton & Hove, DA310117

B62 Teapot

B63 Two vases

Opaque white glass, enamelled
17 x 10cm diameter,
13cm x 8cm diam
South Staffordshire, 1755-60

From the late 17th century, opaque white glass was considered an acceptable substitute for Chinese Dehua blanc-de-chine porcelain. Both baluster-shaped vases are decorated with brightly dressed figures in a rocky landscape.

From a private collection

B64 Large vase and cover

Soft paste porcelain, painted under the glaze
68cm high
Vauxhall factory, London, 1757-60

This massive, extremely rare, baluster-shaped vase is painted in blue with a continuous scene of Chinese village life with a landscape background. Possible print sources have not yet been identified.

From a private collection

B65 Dish

Soft paste porcelain, painted underglaze
18.5 x 18.5cm
Bow factory, London, c1758

This rectangular dish is painted in blue with a wavy border and a design nicknamed 'Golfer and Caddy', copied from a Chinese original, probably representing a travelling scholar whose servant carries his scrolls.

Private collection

B65 Dish

B66 Dish

Soft paste porcelain, painted underglaze
24cm diameter
Bow factory, London, c1758

The plate is painted with a design known as 'the Jumping Boy'. While its Chinese original shows a more realistic scene where the child, wearing an oversized jacket, hops on the ground, the Bow version shows him in mid air! The design is combined here with a border composed of be-ribboned symbols selected from the Eight Treasures, including the artemisia leaf, the dragon pearl and the mirror.

Private collection

B66 Dish

B67 Pair of vases and covers
Soft paste porcelain, enamelled and gilt
33.6cm high
Chelsea, 1759-68

The vases are decorated with an image of exotic birds and a pair of Chinese lovers framed by foliage.

The Bowes Museum, Barnard Castle, Co. Durham, 2004.96.1-2

B68 Pair of pot-pourri vases and covers
Soft paste porcelain, enamelled and gilt
35.5cm high x 15.8cm wide
Chelsea, London, c1760

The gilding on a ground of mazarine blue has been elaborately tooled and burnished to produce different effects, creating compositions of great subtlety. The compositions may owe something to engravings after Boucher, which were used as sources by Meissen modellers.

Salisbury & South Wiltshire Museum

B69 Dish
Soft paste porcelain, painted underglaze
4.8 x 16.7cm
Bow, c1760

Royal Pavilion & Museums, Brighton & Hove, DA 321430

B70 Leaf-shaped dish
Soft paste porcelain, enamelled over the glaze
21cm wide
Worcester, c1760

The centre is decorated with a figure scene sometimes known as 'the Magician'. The male figure is the mirror image of one that was very popular at Worcester and Liverpool, known as 'the Beckoning Chinaman'. (See cat B62.)

The Trustees of the British Museum, 1923,0716.16

B71 Vase and cover
Soft paste porcelain, painted in overglaze colours and gilt
29cm high
Chelsea, c1760

This vase is a rare example of Chelsea's turquoise glaze, used as a ground for painted and incised gilding. The turquoise ground was probably directly inspired by glazes pioneered at Sèvres (see also cat B68). There are exotic birds on one side and, on the other, three children in Chinese dress sit on a lattice-work bench in a Chinese garden with a tame bird behind them.

The Trustees of the British Museum, 1948,1203.60

B72 Vase
Soft paste porcelain, glazed
23.2 x 12.7cm
Chelsea, c1760

The vase has ill-defined dragon-shaped side handles and imitates Chinese blanc-de-chine (see cat B56).

The Trustees of the British Museum, 1887,0307.II.9

B73 Plate
Soft paste porcelain, enamelled overglaze
2.8 x 22.5cm diameter
Bow, c1760

Royal Pavilion & Museums, Brighton & Hove, DAH21.1953

B74 Jug
Soft paste porcelain, enamelled overglaze
26.7cm high
Worcester, c1760

Worcester Porcelain Museum, no 1492

B74 Jug

B75 Saucer
Soft paste porcelain, printed overglaze
12cm diameter
Bow factory, London, c1760

The design was probably drawn by Robert Hancock. Known as Les Garçons Chinois, the exact source for the design is not known but it resembles Pillement's capricci featuring figures on seesaws in landscape settings, used in interior schemes from the 1750s.

Private collection

B75 Saucer

B76 Octagonal plate

Soft paste porcelain, enamel decorated
22cm diameter
Bow factory, London, c1760

Pallant House Gallery, Chichester (Geoffrey Freeman Collection of Bow Porcelain, 1999), no 148

B76 Octagonal plate

B77 Bowl

Soft paste porcelain,
decorated underglaze
8 x 20cm
Bow factory, London, 1762-65

Pallant House Gallery, Chichester (Geoffrey Freeman Collection of Bow Porcelain, 1999), no 99

B77 Bowl

B78 Dish

Soft paste porcelain, enamelled and gilt
16.1 x 20cm
Bow factory, London, c1765

The design of a woman selling haberdashery at an ornate table is taken from plate 32 of Edwards and Darly's New Book of Chinese Designs… *(1754). A copy of this book was found among the papers associated with John Bowcock, clerk to the Bow porcelain warehouse.*

The Victoria & Albert Museum, 310:1-1889

B79 Coffee pot and cover

Soft paste porcelain, painted
under the glaze
20.5 x 15.5cm
Derby, c1765

This coffee pot is decorated with figures loosely based on illustrations in publications by Nieuhof, and Edwards and Darly.

Birmingham Museums and Art Gallery, 1926M737

B80 Coffee cup

Soft paste porcelain,
transfer-printed in blue
9 x 9cm
Derby, (inscribed beneath handle,
with anchor) c1765

This cup is printed with designs known as 'L'Oiseau' and 'La Dame Chinoise'. The former, adapted from a print by Pierre Aveline after Boucher's depiction of 'Air', is from a set of The Four Elements. The exaggerated looping draperies of the tall 'Dame Chinoise' of the latter print recall those featured in Edwards and Darly's New Book of Chinese Designs… *(1754).*

The Trustees of the British Museum, 1929,514.1

B81 Mug

Soft paste porcelain,
enamelled over the glaze
16 x 16cm
Liverpool, Reid factory, c1765

The mug is decorated with a large image of a Chinese fishing boat. A number of similar boats are depicted in views of river traffic at 'Hocsieu' in the so-called Atlas Chinensis *('Arnoldus Montanus', published in England in 1671). A sampan with a similar tented cabin appears on Plate 119 of Edwards and Darly's* New Book of Chinese Designs… *(1754).*

The Trustees of the British Museum, 1940,0401.9

B82 Baluster mug

Soft paste porcelain, enamel decorated
14.5 x 11.3cm
Bow factory, London, c1765

Pallant House Gallery, Chichester (Geoffrey Freeman Collection of Bow Porcelain, 1999), no 165

B82 Baluster mug

B83 Coffee pot

Soft paste porcelain, enamel decorated
17.3 x 11.5cm
Bow factory, London, c1765

Pallant House Gallery, Chichester (Geoffrey Freeman Collection of Bow Porcelain, 1999), no 1149

B83 Coffee pot

B84 Bowl

Soft paste porcelain, painted underglaze
8 x 16.5cm
Worcester, 1765-70

The bowl is painted in blue with a motif from a Chinese pattern of around 1710, from the reign of the Kangxi emperor (1661-1722), a design known as 'The Eloping Bride'. Pseudo-Chinese Buddhist symbols are applied on the footring.

Worcester Porcelain Museum, no 260

B84 Bowl

B85 Teapot and coffee pot

Soft paste porcelain, printed and enamelled overglaze and gilt
Teapot 13.5 x 19cm,
coffee pot 17 x 17.5cm
Worcester, c1770

The teapot and coffee pot are printed with a design known as 'The Chinese Family'.

Royal Pavilion & Museums, Brighton & Hove, DA310096, DA321331

B86 Vase

Soft paste porcelain, painted underglaze
21.2 x 11.7cm
Worcester, c1770

The vase is based on a Chinese original; such vases were often produced in threes to form a garniture.

Royal Pavilion & Museums, Brighton & Hove, DA321443

B87 Mug

Soft paste porcelain, printed underglaze
13.5 x 14.5cm
Worcester, 1770-75

This large cider mug features three designs after Pillement from The Ladies Amusement *(1758-60). Two popular designs, 'La Pêche' and 'La Promenade Chinoise' (pl.148) are joined by 'Temple Bells' (pl.37) which first appeared on the title page of Pillement's* New Book of Chinese Ornaments *(1755).*

Worcester Porcelain Museum, no 401

B87 Mug

B88 Mug

Soft paste porcelain, printed underglaze
8.8 x 9.5cm
Worcester, 1770-75

The mug has two designs after Pillement from The Ladies Amusement. *(See cat B87.)*

Royal Pavilion & Museums, Brighton & Hove, DA321450

B89 Mug

Soft paste porcelain, printed underglaze
8 x 9cm
Caughley, 1770-75 (marked 'C')

The Caughley factory has here used the same chinoiserie sources as cat B88.

Royal Pavilion & Museums, Brighton & Hove, DAH44.1995

B90 Mug

Soft paste porcelain
12cm high
Lowestoft, Suffolk, 1770-75

Brian Haughton Gallery, London

B91 Plate

Soft paste porcelain,
enamelled overglaze
3 x 22.5cm diameter
Worcester, 1770-75
(marked with gold 'C')

The plate is enamelled with a design based on a Chinese pattern from the reign of the Kangxi Emperor (1661-1722).

Royal Pavilion & Museums, Brighton & Hove

B92 Dish
Hard paste porcelain,
painted underglaze
16cm diameter
China, c1700

The dish has a central design of be-ribboned Buddhist symbols called 'Precious Objects', from the reign of the Kangxi Emperor (1661-1722). Chinese prototypes were closely copied by decorators at the Worcester factory (see B93).

Private collection

B92 Dish

B93 Plate
Soft paste porcelain, painted underglaze
22.8cm diameter
Worcester factory, 1770-80

This lobed-edged plate has a design called 'the Hundred Antiques', closely based on Chinese prototypes featuring Buddhist 'Precious Objects'. The plate is decorated on the reverse with pseudo-Chinese characters (see B92).

Royal Pavilion & Museums, Brighton & Hove, DA320405

B94 Plate
Soft paste porcelain, painted underglaze
21cm diameter
Worcester factory, 1770-80

This plate is painted with a design called 'the Fan-panelled Landscape'. It is closely based on a Bow porcelain design of c1760. The plate is decorated on the reverse with pseudo-Chinese characters.

Royal Pavilion & Museums, Brighton & Hove, DA322677

B95 Plate
Soft paste porcelain, painted underglaze
17.6cm diameter
Worcester factory, 1770-80

This plate has a design known as 'the Kangxi Lotus'. It is decorated on the reverse with a be-ribboned mirror, one of the Eight (Ordinary) Buddhist Treasures.

Royal Pavilion & Museums, Brighton & Hove, DA321449

B96 Tea bowl and saucer
Soft paste porcelain, printed underglaze
Bowl 4.3 x 7.4cm,
saucer 2.8 x 12.5cm
Worcester, 1775-85

The design, known as the 'Mother and Child', may be taken from a Chinese original.

Royal Pavilion & Museums, Brighton & Hove, DA321433, DAH478.1953

B97 Plate
Soft paste porcelain, painted underglaze
22.7cm diameter
Possibly Masons, Staffordshire c1790

Royal Pavilion & Museums, Brighton & Hove, DA321429

B98 Pair of vases
Hard paste porcelain enamelled black and decorated in gold and platinum, with gilt bronze mounts and gilt bases
41.9 x 34.3cm
Sèvres, France, 1789-92

This extraordinary pair of pot-pourri vases is enamelled black, imitating lacquer and fitted with gilt bronze mounts, including a coronet and a shallow canopy at the shoulder, hung with bells. The side handles terminate in split Greek keys on which dragons perch. The vases are decorated with chinoiserie caprices in two shades of gold and platinum. One seesaw scene is taken directly from a plate engraved by J J Avril in Pillement's Cahier des Balançoires Chinoises *(1773), one of a number of themed albums of his designs published in the 1770s. The vases were probably purchased in Paris in 1815 for George, Prince of Wales, by his 'china man', Robert Fogg. They were displayed at Carlton House before being sent to the Royal Pavilion in 1819.*

The Royal Collection, RCIN 2347.1-2

B99 Pair of vases
Hard paste porcelain, with gilt bronze mounts and marble bases
46.7cm and 48.9cm high
China, late 18th century; mounts, London 1807

One of the unmatched vases is glazed copper red, the other has a light blue crackled glaze and they sit on red and green marble plinths, respectively. Both are fitted with magnificent chased dragons at the neck and sit in lotus flower cups, all in gilt bronze, supplied by B L Vulliamy in 1807. Thirteen craftsmen were involved in making the mounts, which cost the princely sum of £85.19s.11d. They were probably intended for the Chinese Drawing Room at Carlton House. In 1811 they were moved to the Bow Room and in 1819 they were sent to the Royal Pavilion.

The Royal Collection, RCIN 187 & 188

B100 Pagoda

Hard paste porcelain and bone china with gilt bronze mounts and scagliola plinth
376 x 84cm
China, c1810; English additions and mounts, 1817

This pagoda is one of six supplied for the Music Room of the Royal Pavilion in 1817 at a cost of £2,004 by the dealer Robert Fogg, who added the bells, fish, dragons and lion dogs to the tiers of famille rose porcelain. B L Vulliamy provided the pierced galleries, mounts and snake-entwined arrowhead finial, all designed by Frederick Crace. The bone china base, made by Spode, is enamelled with panels copied from Chinese export watercolours and Henry Westmacott supplied the plinth. This pagoda and its pair flanked the fireplace; four larger ones stood before the window piers. Taken as a group, the Music Room porcelain pagodas represent the acme of taste for chinoiserie in Regency England.

The Royal Collection, RCIN 2400.1

B101 The 'Kylin' clock

Hard paste porcelain, with gilt bronze mounts
111.7 x 81.3 x 36.9cm
Chinese porcelain late 17th-18th century; French clock c 1750; mounts and base, London 1821-23

The clock was assembled in France at an unknown date. King George IV purchased it around 1820 for the Royal Pavilion and had B L Vulliamy replace the movement a year later. The movement, inserted into the base of a 17th century Chinese famille verte bowl (turned on its side), is flanked by a pair of turquoise Buddhist lions (incorrectly known as 'kylins'). The porcelain panels in the base are also Chinese. The Japanese budhai group, above the clock, is surrounded by gilt bronze sunflowers, designed by Robert Jones and supplied by Samuel Parker c1821-23. The clock was integral to Jones's decorative ensemble for the Saloon of the Royal Pavilion.

The Royal Collection, RCIN 2867

B102 Plate

Soft paste porcelain, enamelled overglaze and gilt
19.5cm diameter
Chamberlains Worcester factory, c1800

This plate is enamelled with a design known as 'Dragon in Compartments' based on a Chinese pattern from the reign of the Kangxi Emperor (1661-1722).

Royal Pavilion & Museums, Brighton & Hove, DAH397.1953

B103 Plate

Soft paste porcelain, enamelled overglaze and gilt
23.5cm diameter
Worcester porcelain factory, 1811-12

This plate, from one of the extraordinary services commissioned by the Prince Regent, is decorated in a rich Imari style. Three reserves are enamelled with abundant chinoiserie gardens around the Regent's coat of arms in the centre.

Worcester Porcelain Museum, no 1642

B104 Pages from Pattern Book

Ink and watercolour on paper
Chamberlains Worcester factory, 1811

A selection of designs for services commissioned by the Prince Regent from Chamberlain's Worcester factory.

Worcester Porcelain Museum

B105 Dish

Soft paste porcelain, printed underglaze
16.5cm diameter
Spode factory, Stoke-on-Trent, c1815 (pattern 2414)

The ferocious images of dragons appear to be closely based on Chinese prototypes.

Private collection

B105 Dish

B106 Pair of monumental vases and covers

Stone china, printed, enamelled and gilt Each 150cm high
C J Mason & Co, Fenton, Staffordshire, 1830-45

Each vase is printed with Chinese fan-shaped reserves and decorative bands on a sea-green ground adorned with pink flowers. Each reserve is decorated with oriental figures and animals, cloud forms and pagodas in landscape settings. The pagoda finials may have been inspired by William Chambers's pagoda in Kew Gardens, designed in 1762.

Brian Haughton Gallery, London

B106 Pair of monumental vases and covers

FIGURES

B107 Figure
Earthenware, glazed
10.5 x 14cm
China, c1700

This figure is modelled as Budai, the Chinese god of prosperity and contentment. He sits cross-legged with a peach in one hand, symbol of springtime and longevity. Such figures were closely copied in Europe and at the Chelsea factory in London (see cat B108).

Royal Pavilion & Museums, Brighton & Hove, DA322203

B108 Figure
Soft paste porcelain
9 x 8.7cm high
Chelsea, London, c1746

This small figure is modelled as Budai (see cat B107). The plump, bare-bellied figure sits cross-legged with a pearl in one hand, one of the Eight Treasures. This figure is closely modelled on a Chinese Dehua blanc-de-chine model; the Elector of Saxony owned several examples in the late 17th century.

Private collection

B109 Figure of Guan Yin
Hard paste porcelain
19.5 x 12cm
China, c1700

The seated figure, bowed in meditation, represents Guan Yin, Goddess of Mercy and Compassion, highly revered in Chinese Buddhism. The uncoloured figure was made in Dehua porcelain, known as blanc-de-chine, in China's Fujian Province.

Pallant House Gallery, Chichester (Brian Winch, 1993), no 0756

B109 Figure of Guan Yin

B110 Figure of Guan Yin
Soft paste porcelain, glazed
12 x 9cm
Chelsea, c1750

There is no doubt that the figure represents Guan Yin, the Chinese Mother goddess, and it was probably copied from an example of Fujian blanc-de-chine porcelain. However the twin-horned head-veil and the plump face of the goddess make her look more like a European peasant woman.

The Trustees of the British Museum, 1938,0314.103

B111 Figure of Lü Dongbin
Glazed soft paste porcelain
17.2 x 7.1cm
Bristol, 1750 (moulded 'Bristoll 1750')

This is a rare figure of Lü Dongbin (or Lu Tung Pin), an 8th century scholar and recluse, who became one of the Eight Daoist Immortals. He carries a fly whisk and is usually shown carrying a sword on his back, awarded when he overcame ten temptations.

Victoria & Albert Museum, C.1300-1924

B112 Figure of Zhonglí Quán
White saltglazed stoneware
19 x 8cm
Staffordshire c1750

This figure represents the chief of the Eight Daoist Immortals, who is said to have lived under the Zhou Dynasty (1122-249 BC) and is thought to have learned the elixir of life. He is shown with his emblem, a fan, with which he is said to revive the souls of the dead. The figure is based on a Chinese original.

Victoria & Albert Museum, 414.859:1-1885

B113 Figure of Shou Lao

Lead-glazed earthenware, coloured with manganese and cobalt oxide
8cm x 6.7cm
Wheildon factory, Staffordshire c1750

This figure, based on a Chinese original represents Shou-lao or Shou-xing, the Daoist star-god of long life and luck. He carries the pántáo peach of immortality and a piece of língzhi (sacred fungus) and is accompanied by a crane and a stag.

Victoria & Albert Museum, 414.1042-1885

B114 Figure group: Boy on a Buffalo

Lead-glazed earthenware, coloured with manganese oxide
18.5 x 24cm
Staffordshire c1750

The group is probably based on a Chinese original. In China the ox or buffalo is the emblem of spring, agriculture and physical strength, and is revered for its contribution to ploughing and milling.

Victoria & Albert Museum, 414.1046A-1885

B115 Pair of busts

Soft paste porcelain
Male: 28.5 x 12.5cm
Female: 26.5 x 13cm
Bow factory, London, c1750

These rare and exotic busts (at least one other pair is known) were formerly known as the 'Roumanian (or Hungarian) Minister and his wife' although the Bowcock memorandum book for April 1756 refers to Chinese heads. They have strongly modelled faces with European features and almond eyes, and are exotically dressed in fitted robes with heavy embroidery and frogging, their caps fringed with bobbles.

Pallant House Gallery, Chichester (Geoffrey Freeman Collection of Bow Porcelain, 1999), no 188

B115 Pair of busts

B116 Figure group: Ki Mâo Sâo

Soft paste porcelain, enamel decorated
17 x 26.3cm
Bow factory, London, 1750-52

The group is based on Aubert's engraving after Watteau's image of the goddess Ki Mâo Sâo, published around 1730 (see cat F4). The lightness and wit of the original, that toyed subversively with the image of a courtesan and the worship of idols, is lost in the heaviness of the clay and the decision of the 'Muses' modeller' to play the scene for slapstick amusement. Beneath the goddess's seat an oval reserve is inscribed in puce with Chinese characters, assumed to be fake. John Finlay has revealed that it is part of a real phrase that reads 'Genuine Spring Yunqian [tea]' probably carefully transcribed from a tea chest.

Pallant House Gallery, Chichester (Geoffrey Freeman Collection of Bow Porcelain, 1999), no 195

B117 Figure group: Sense of Feeling

Glazed, soft paste porcelain
23.5 x 14.9cm
Derby c1750

The Sense of Feeling is modelled as an elderly Chinese man. The composition may be based on unidentified prints of 'les cinq Sens par différents amusements chinois' after Boucher, advertised in the Mercure in 1740. In addition, John Mallet suggested (in 2002) that the modeller of this and other 'dry-edge' Derby groups was not Andrew Planché but the renowned sculptor Agostino Carlini (c1718-90), who was working in London in the early 1750s.

Victoria & Albert Museum, 414.140-1885

B118 Figure group: Hearing or Sight

Soft paste porcelain, enamelled over the glaze
20 x 17.5cm
Derby, 1750-52

There has been much confusion over the identity of this very rare figure group, one of five representing the Senses. Probably based on the same source as cat B117, the male figure holds a tight scroll but artefacts held by the female figure are often missing, as they are here. When present they are interpreted variously as the mouthpiece of a wind instrument, a lyre or a mirror, leading to the group being said to represent either Hearing or Sight. As with cat B117, the modeller may have been Agostino Carlini.

The Trustees of the British Museum, 1938,0314.88

B116 Figure group: Ki Mâo Sâo

B119 Figure group: Sense of Smell

Soft paste porcelain, enamelled
over the glaze
21.8cm high
Derby, c1752

The Sense of Smell is modelled as an adult Chinese man. For the probable source and the modeller, see cat nos B117 and B118.

The Bowes Museum, Barnard Castle, Co. Durham, 2004.122

B120 Figure

Soft paste porcelain, enamelled
17.8cm high
Chelsea, c1754

Two flamboyant Chinese figures were produced during Chelsea's Red Anchor period. He sports a large moustache and tugs at his long beard while striking a theatrical pose reminiscent of Meissen Commedia dell'Arte figures.

Lent by Amgueddfa Cymru - National Museum Wales

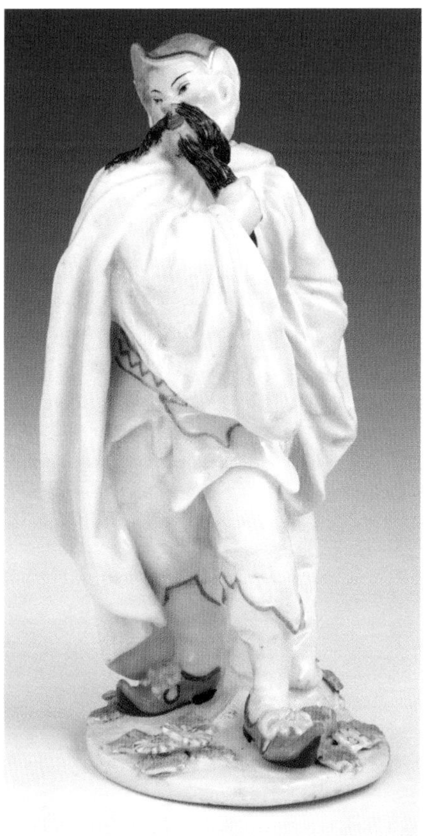

B120 Figure

B121 Figure

Soft paste porcelain,
enamelled overglaze
11.3 x 6cm
Chelsea, 1754-5

This figure is probably copied from a Meissen model.

Royal Pavilion & Museums, Brighton & Hove, DAH71.1990

B122 Pair of posy vases

Soft paste porcelain, enamelled
over the glaze
Male figure: 17.7 x 14.6cm
Female figure: 18.6 x 12cm
Chelsea, c1760

These vases may have been modelled by the talented Fleming, Joseph Willems (1715-66), who was working at Chelsea from the 1750s, or they may be based on figures modelled by Reinicke for Meissen in the 1740s.

Birmingham Museums & Art Gallery, on loan from Lord Phillimore

B123 Figure

Soft paste porcelain, enamelled
over the glaze
24 x 16.5cm
Derby, c1760

This piece was originally designed as a watch holder with two protuberances to support watch and chain. Other examples show a small boy crouched at the base, leading to the group's nickname of 'Sorcerer and Apprentice'.

The Trustees of the British Museum, 1938,0314.102

Furniture and Furnishings

C1 Panel from the Heaven Room, Bolsover Castle
Oak, painted with landscape vignettes in shell gold and varnished
43.2cm x 27.2cm
Anglo-Netherlandish, c.1616-19

Structurally complete in c.1616 and decorated c.1616-19 to a scheme devised by Sir Charles Cavendish (1653-1617), the Heaven Room in the Little Castle at Bolsover contains possibly the earliest surviving chinoiserie decoration in Britain. Intended as a bedroom closet, the panelling in the room was probably painted by an Anglo-Netherlandish artist familiar with continental pattern books. Shell gold, an extremely expensive preparation of gold leaf bound in glue and stored in mussel shells (hence the name), was used to outline the delicate landscape vignettes. The windmill design on the exhibited panel does not look particularly oriental, but the dark green ground with high gloss varnish was intended to simulate Chinese or Japanese lacquer.

English Heritage (The Heaven Closet, Little Castle, Bolsover Castle, Derbyshire)

C1 Panel from the Heaven Room, Bolsover Castle

Main image: C16 *Chinese drummer-boy clock,* bronze, chased, gilt, and painted; movement by Charles Frodsham. French, c.1787-90

C2 Cabinet
Oak and (?) eucalyptus, painted, silvered and gilded
66 x 60 x 30cm
Possibly English, c.1620

This puzzling cabinet is probably contemporary with the chinoiserie panelling from Bolsover Castle (see cat. C1). It belongs to a small group which may have been made in the same workshop; a ballot box belonging to the Saddlers' Company dated 1619 gives an approximate date (see p.15). Furniture of this type may have been called 'China Worke' in inventories; the shape seems to have been inspired by small Japanese export cabinets of the late 16th century. The decoration, richly painted in gold and silver with arabesques and 'oriental' figures, resembles in some respects Milanese damascening, which might imply the Middle East rather than the Far East.

Leeds Museums & Galleries (Temple Newsam), 1971.0034

C2 Cabinet

C3 Four sections of a Coromandel screen
Coloured and incised lacquer
285 x 189.5cm
Chinese, Kangxi, 1662-1722

The screen is decorated and incised with scenes from a famous Chinese story of the Qing dynasty known as the Dream of the Red Chambers, attributed to Cao Zhan. It is a tale of and memorial to the women the author knew. Made in northern or central China, the screen follows the usual arrangement of a long panel with narrative scenes above smaller ones with auspicious Chinese symbols. Such screens are hybrid creations, combining Chinese, Japanese and even Western design motifs. They were very expensive and, when imported, were frequently cut up and applied to furniture (see cat. C6). They were called Coromandel screens because they came to England from China via Coromandel on the Madras Coast.

Leeds Museums & Galleries (Temple Newsam), 1940.0021

C3 Coromandel screen

C4 Cabinet on stand
Pine and oak, japanned
226 x 54cm
English, c.1690-1700

The cabinet is japanned inside and out with partly raised chinoiserie scenes in gilt on a black ground with silvered, red and brown details. As well as being a branch of furniture manufacture, the 'curious and ingenious art and mystery of japanning' was particularly recommended for women and amateurs. The crane on the inside of the left-hand door is reminiscent of pl. 10 of Stalker and Parker's Treatise of Japaning and Varnishing *(1688). The cabinet would have been a luxurious object, possibly standing in a bedroom; its gleaming black and gold surface and gilt metal mounts enlivened candle-lit rooms. The stretchers were intended to support Chinese porcelain vases.*

Leeds Museums & Galleries (Temple Newsam), 1959.0012

C4 Cabinet on stand

C5 Cabinet on stand

Pine and oak, japanned ivory ground
203 x 119.5 x 60cm
English, c .1690-1700

This cabinet on a stand is the largest and grandest of a group of four similar ivory ground cabinets probably made in the same London workshop. Ivory coloured japanning is very rare; instead of imitating black and gold lacquer, it here resembles polychrome decoration on Chinese porcelain and painted silks. The silvered cresting and stand, carved with themes of Plenty, are also rare survivals; the cresting has small brackets for Chinese porcelain vases reminiscent of the designs of Daniel Marot.

The Holburne Museum of Art, Bath, 2005.3

C5 Cabinet on stand

C6 Coromandel lacquer chest

Walnut, oak, pine and lacquer
74 x 102 x 54cm
English, c.1730

Chinese coromandel lacquer with carved designs (cat C3) was often cut up to form chests and cabinets. Stalker and Parker (cat E3), writing in 1688, referred to those who made 'new Cabinets out of old Skreens ... but never consider the situation of their figures; so that ... you may observe the finest hodgpodg and medley of Men and Trees turned topsie turvie'. This chest, formerly at Castle Howard, is probably associated with the 3rd Earl of Carlisle (1669-1738), who had a taste for opulent display, rich materials, Vanderbank tapestries and parade furniture.

Leeds Museums & Galleries (Temple Newsam), 1992.0003

C6 Coromandel lacquer chest

C7 Armchair by Giles Grendey (1693-1780)

Japanned beech
113 x 75 x 52cm
English, c.1735-40

One of a suite of chairs supplied to the Duke of Infantado, Lazcano Castle Northern Spain. Styled to appeal to the Spanish taste for opulence, each chair in the set is enriched with chinoiseries in gold and silver with black details on a scarlet japanned ground. The oriental figures standing beneath umbrellas against a landscape of feathery trees could derive from motifs on Chinese export lacquer or porcelain.

Leeds Museums & Galleries (Temple Newsam), 1970.0010

C7 Armchair by Giles Grendey (1693-1780)

C8 Armchair by William (c.1703–63) and John (1729-96) Linnell

Japanned beech
103.5 x 67.5 x 66cm
English, c.1754

Part of a suite of furniture in the Chinese style supplied to the 4th Duke of Beaufort (1709-1759) by the Linnells for the Chinese Bedroom at Badminton House, Gloucestershire. Possibly the earliest surviving bedroom suite, it seems likely that the chinoiserie style was selected by the Duchess. William Linnell was one of the first cabinetmakers to adopt the style; he had already created a Chinese house at Woburn for the Duke of Bedford in 1749.

The fretwork at the back of the chair derives in part from 'Chinese double brac'd paling' published in William Halfpenny's New Designs for Chinese Temples *(1750).*

Victoria & Albert Museum, W34-1990

C8 Armchair by William (c.1703–63) and John (1729-96) Linnell

C9 Chair attributed to Wright and Elwick of Wakefield, Yorkshire (fl. 1747-1771)

Mahogany, partly gilded; contemporary needlework seat
107.5 x 60.5 x 63.5cm
English, c.1755

This vigorous and idiosyncratic chair may have been supplied to Peregrine Bertie, 19th Baron Willoughby de Eresby, 3rd Duke of Ancaster (1714-1778) for the Chinese 'breakfasting closet' (now the Birdcage Room) at Grimsthorpe Castle, Lincolnshire. It has been attributed to Richard Wright and Edward Elwick of Yorkshire and to William Hallett of London. The former attribution seems likely as the Yorkshire cabinetmakers seem to have specialised in furniture with an oriental influence and the chair has provincial mannerisms, particularly the archaic gilding. The pagoda cresting and the Chinese fret on the seat rails may derive from Rural Architecture in the Chinese Taste by William and John Halfpenny (3rd ed. 1755) and the interlaced back is related to designs in William de la Cour's First Book of Ornaments *(1741).*

Private collection

C9 Chair attributed to Wright and Elwick of Wakefield, Yorkshire (fl. 1747-1771)

C10 Looking glass

Wood frame, carved and gilt
180 x 104cm
English, c.1755-60

It is not known whether this looking glass, from Halnaby Hall, Yorkshire, was commissioned for the house. It would certainly have been a match for the exceptional rococo plasterwork. The full-blooded chinoiserie motifs can be traced to such sources as M Lock and H Copland's New Book of Ornaments *(1752). The looking glass was re-gilded in the 1960s.*

The Bowes Museum, Barnard Castle, Co Durham, FW55

C10 Looking glass

C11 Armchair

Mahogany and beech
95 x 67.5 x 57cm
English, c.1755-65

The shaped arms are filled with a Chinese lattice paling centred on an octagonal panel and the legs are enriched with blind Chinese fret. The lattice motif could have been adapted from a number of sources, most probably William Halfpenny's Twenty New Designs of Chinese Lattice, *1750.*

Leeds Museums & Galleries (Temple Newsam), 1966.0016.0001

C11 Armchair

C12 Day Bed attributed to Thomas Chippendale (1718-1779)

Mahogany, painted silk; modern upholstery
279.4 x 241.3 x 91.4cm
English, c.1758

One of a pair of unique day beds in the form of miniature chinoiserie garden pavilions commissioned by the Hon Francis Charteris, later 7th Earl of Wemyss, and his wife Lady Katherine, for Amisfield, East Lothian (dem 1928) and now at Stanway, Gloucestershire. The day beds have been attributed to Thomas Chippendale because both Francis Charteris and Lady Katherine were subscribers to Chippendale's Gentleman and Cabinet Maker's Director *(1754) and because the canopy is similar to pl. XXVI of the* Director. *The canopy, or pagoda roof, which is lined with Chinese silk, and the miniature temple or roof gazebo, may derive from pl. I of William and John Halfpenny's* Chinese and Gothic Architecture Properly Ornamented *(1752).*

The Earl of Wemyss and March, KT

C12 Day Bed attributed to Thomas Chippendale (1718-1779)

C13 Chair in the style of Thomas Chippendale (1718-1779)

Mahogany
100 x 61 x 54cm
English, c.1760

*From a set of six. The back splat is close to Chippendale's design for 'ribband back chairs' in pl. XVI of the Gentleman and Cabinet Maker's Director (1754) and the open fret front legs are similar to pl XXIV. The pendant low relief tassels might have been seen by contemporaries as a chinoiserie motif. The open fret could be gothic or Chinese; it illustrates William Whitehead's 'happy mixture' of styles (*The World, *1754).*

Private collection

C13 Chair in the style of Thomas Chippendale (1718-1779)

C14 Tea table in the style of Thomas Chippendale (1718-1779)

Mahogany
76 x 90 x 61cm
English, c.1760

The general form of the table derives from pl. 34 of Chippendale's Director *(see cat F13), where they are described as 'China or Breakfast Tables'. Similar examples can be seen in the third edition (1762, pl. LI). The Chinese fret on the gallery is clear, though the apron, legs and stretchers combine chinoiserie, gothic and rococo motifs.*

Private collection

C14 Tea table in the style of Thomas Chippendale (1718-1779)

C15 Wardrobe by Thomas Chippendale (1718-1779)

Pine, beech and birch japanned and painted green
167.5 x 136 x 62cm
English, c.1768-70

Part of a suite of furniture supplied by Chippendale to the actor-manager David Garrick (1717-1779) for his villa at Hampton, Surrey. The rural and informal atmosphere of Garrick's villa probably suggested painted or japanned rather than veneered or gilded furniture. The 'rustic' chinoiserie landscapes were probably the choice of Mrs Garrick. The Garricks' bedroom and dressing room was hung with Chinese paper and Indian chintz and on the first floor was an early example of a Chinese drawing room. The wardrobe has suffered from extensive overpainting.

Victoria & Albert Museum, W23-1917

C16 Chinese drummer-boy clock

Bronze, chased, gilt, and painted; movement by Charles Frodsham (fl. 1834-71)
73.6 x 34.3 x 19.5cm
French, c.1787-90

Like the Weisweiler table (cat C17), this clock may have been designed by Dominique Daguerre. The original movement, by Charles-Guillaume Manière, was replaced in c 1870 by Charles Frodsham. The tasselled base of gilt bronze was added by B L Vulliamy in 1811. The clock formed part of the furnishings of the Prince of Wales's Chinese Drawing Room at Carlton House; it was sent to the Royal Pavilion in 1819 and was in the Lord Steward's apartments in 1829. The Chinese figure, perched on a range of craggy rocks, is a perfect expression of European chinoiserie where even time, it seems, was subject to the whims of a jocular mandarin.

The Royal Collection, RCIN 2868

C16 Chinese drummer-boy clock

C17 Pier table by Adam Weisweiler (1744-1820)

Ebony veneer, gilt bronze mounts, mirrored glass panels, marble shelves and top. Stamped A Weisweiler
91 x 175 x 52.7cm
French, c.1787-90

Probably designed by Dominique Daguerre, the Prince of Wales's furniture adviser and marchand-mercier (supplier of luxury goods), this table, and a plainer companion, were supplied by Daguerre for the Chinese Drawing Room at Carlton House, London, created by Henry Holland and Daguerre c.1787-90. The table, though of conventional Louis XVI form, is, with its Chinese caryatid figures, dragons, peacocks, drapery and bamboo, in the most advanced Parisian chinoiserie taste. Both Weisweiler tables were despatched to Brighton Pavilion in 1819, where, prior to their installation in the Music Room Gallery, copies were made by Edward Bailey of Bailey and Sanders.

The Royal Collection, RCIN 181

C17 Pier table by Adam Weisweiler (1744-1820)

C18 Armchair by François Hervé (fl. 1781-96)

Beech, carved and gilded
102.9 x 59.7 x 62.5 cm
Anglo-French, c.1790-92

As with catalogue nos C16 and 17 it is likely that Dominique Daguerre had a hand in the design of this chair, one of a set supplied in 1790 for the Chinese Drawing Room at Carlton House. The seated Chinaman on a cushion on the top rail was added in 1792 and the chair was gilded by Sefferin Nelson. The remarkable pierced chair frame is a technical feat unparalleled in English or French chair making. When the chairs were moved to the Royal Pavilion in 1819 they were placed in the Yellow Drawing Room. Following the remodelling of that room in 1821 and the creation of the Music Room Gallery, umbrella-topped columns with entwined snakes were inserted which deliberately echoed the serpent motif on the legs of the Hervé chairs.

The Royal Collection, RCIN 481

C18 Armchair by François Hervé (fl. 1781-96)

C19 Hanging lantern

Painted and lacquered wood, iron and glass
170cm
Chinese with English additions, c.1802

Almost certainly supplied by John or Frederick Crace in c.1802 for P F Robinson's new dining room at the Royal Pavilion, the lantern is partly Chinese and partly English. The original painted glass panels and parts of the wooden framework are Chinese export, but the lantern appears to have been assembled in England where the iron framework was added. By 1826, when an inventory of the Pavilion was made, the lantern (one of four) was in store and was described as having 'japanned scarlet borders and gilt decorations panelled in ground glass painted after the Mythology'. After 1864, when the lantern was returned to the Pavilion by Queen Victoria, the glass panels were overpainted with motifs after William Alexander's Costume of China *(1805) and the framework was painted green.*

Royal Pavilion & Museums, Brighton & Hove

C20 Dragon roundel

Pine, silvered and painted
130cm (diam)
English, c.1815

Branded G R PAVILION on the reverse, the roundel is possibly the one referred to in the 1815 Crace accounts for the Royal Pavilion under 'Entrance Hall - 1 large Dragon silvered and painted in proper colours'. It functioned as a ceiling rose.

Royal Pavilion & Museums, Brighton & Hove

C21 Pair of vases by Jennens and Bettridge

Papier-mâché with ormolu mounts
97cm
English, c.1830

Commissioned by Isabella, Lady Hertford (1760-1834) for the Chinese Drawing Room at Temple Newsam, Leeds, these vases were probably intended to extend a set of famille noire *porcelain vases in similar mounts. The papier-mâché bodies have been japanned to imitate black glazed Kangxi (1662-1722) Chinese porcelain. Jennens and Bettridge 'Japanners in Ordinary to His Majesty' were the best-known papier-mâché manufacturers of the time. The ormolu mounts may have been made in the workshops of Edward Holmes Baldock (1777-1845).*

Leeds Museums & Galleries (Temple Newsam), 2002.0083

C21 Pair of vases by Jennens and Bettridge

C22 Dragon chair carved by Thomas Wilkinson Wallis of Hull (1821- 1903)

Composition and gesso, gilded
114 x 89 x 78cm
English, c.1841

In 1784 a Chinese Drawing Room was created by William Constable at Burton Constable, near Hull. In 1840 Thomas Ward of Hull (1782-1850) remodelled and re-fitted the room, but left the carving of this remarkable chair to his pupil Thomas Wilkinson Wallis, who based it on sketches made in the Royal Pavilion, Brighton, by Marianne, Lady Clifford Constable (died 1862) whilst on a visit with her husband, Sir Thomas, in c 1827. Coincidentally, the dragon formed part of the crest of the Clifford Constable family. The 1840s chinoiserie scheme in the Chinese Room is a late example of the style.

Burton Constable Foundation

C22 Dragon chair carved by Thomas Wilkinson Wallis of Hull (1821- 1903)

C23 Bench designed by Philip Lockwood (1821-1908)

Oak, stained and gilded
97 x 228 x 58cm
English, c.1864-5

On 19 September 1864 the Borough Surveyor, Philip Lockwood, submitted a design for public seating in the Banqueting Room and Music Room of the Royal Pavilion. Samuel Ireland of Western Road, Brighton, manufactured the eight benches at a cost of £250 and delivered them in 1865. The Lockwood benches form a most interesting and rare example of High Victorian chinoiserie.

Royal Pavilion & Museums, Brighton & Hove

C24 Cabinet on stand designed by Norman Shaw (1831-1912)

Malayan pine with red stain and gold gesso
174 x 127 x 42cm
English, c.1875-7

Designed by the architect Norman Shaw, made by W H Lascelles and decorated by J Aldam Heaton, this cabinet exemplifies Victorian eclecticism at its best. The form is inspired by Spanish 17th century prototypes, but the gilt gesso door panels, by the decorator and art furniture manufacturer, Aldam Heaton, are influenced by Chinese or Japanese lacquer. The red stained wood, again suggestive of lacquer, was probably suggested by W H Lascelles, one of Shaw's builders and an expert on joinery.

Private collection on loan to Leeds Museums & Galleries (Lotherton Hall)

C25 Sofa

Mahogany with chinoiserie silk upholstery
85 x 137 x 57cm
English, late 19th century

The sofa was probably made using pieces from an 18th century chair. It has chinoiserie blind fret legs.

Royal Pavilion & Museums, Brighton & Hove, H1948.21

C26 Buddhist lion

Chinese hardwood, gilded
27.5cm
Chinese, 19th century

Made specifically for export to the west, such lions were referred to as 'Dogs of Fo' (Fo means Buddha), a term coined by 19th century dealers and connoisseurs. Such figures, more usually in porcelain, were frequently used to evoke an idea of China in western 20th century rooms.

Royal Pavilion & Museums, Brighton & Hove, WA505650

C27 Cabinet on stand by Ernest Gimson (1864-1919)

Veneered walnut and ebony with gelt gesso
200 x 119 x 47cm
English, c.1902

Made for the smoking room at Pinbury Park, Gloucestershire, the seat of Earl Bathurst, this is an early product of Gimson's Daneway workshops. The ebony stand is indebted in a general way to Far Eastern lacquer tables, and the cabinet, though based partly on English late 17th century examples, has a verticality of outline similar to oriental furniture. The gilt gesso panels were made by Gimson, probably with the involvement of the workshop manager, Peter Waals. This extremely sophisticated cabinet anticipates high style furniture of the 1920s and 1930s.

Victoria & Albert Museum, W27-1977

C27 Cabinet on stand by Ernest Gimson (1864-1919)

C28 Four post bed

Japanned wood
221 x 150 x 206cm
English, c.1920-30

Little is known about this remarkable bed. It was donated to the Royal Pavilion in 1951 and displayed in the King's Bedroom from 1951-2007. The bed is japanned with foliage, landscape and pagoda motifs in gold on a black ground reminiscent of late 17th century chinoiseries. The mid 1920s saw a revival of interest in chinoiserie. Decorating firms such as Lenygon and Morant, Keebles or White Allom could have provided a bed such as this.

Royal Pavilion & Museums, Brighton & Hove, DA340301

C29 Gramophone manufactured by Edison Bell

Mahogany veneer japanned with chinoiseries
113 x 71 x 53cm
English, c.1920-30

Known as the 'Japanese Lacquer Pedestal Model no 248', this gramophone is in a Queen Anne Revival style. The opening front is japanned with pagodas and fishing figures.

Royal Pavilion & Museums, Brighton & Hove, DATMP000038

C30 Gramophone manufactured by the Columbia Gramophone Company Ltd

Wood frame, japanned with scarlet lacquer
63 (open) x 47 x 54.5cm
English, c.1922-1931

The raised gesso and gilded figures recall early 18th century chinoiseries.

Stephen Calloway

C30 Gramophone manufactured by the Columbia Gramophone Company Ltd

Costume, Textiles and Fans

D1 Woman's bodice

Silk satin with silk stitch quilting embroidered with chinoiseries
61 x 36cm
English, late 17th century

The designs include squirrels and birds reminiscent of chinoiseries in Stalker and Parker's Treatise of Japaning and Varnishing *(1688). The seated couple taking tea is an early instance of the association of tea drinking with chinoiserie. The design was probably provided by professional pattern drawers.*

Birmingham Museums & Art Gallery, 2005.0374

D2 Attributed to John Vanderbank (fl. 1689-1717)

Tapestry, woven in wool and silk with chinoiseries
274 x 90.5cm
English, Soho, c.1700

Vanderbank was the most distinguished tapestry weaver of his time. As Chief Arras-Maker of the Great Wardrobe (a department of the Royal Household situated in Soho), he supplied tapestries 'after the Indian manner' to Kensington Palace in 1690. Tapestries related to the present example are at Belton House, Lincolnshire, the V&A and Yale. Motifs, frequently and indiscriminately re-used, derived from a variety of sources: Indian and Turkish miniatures, Coromandel lacquer screens, and travel books such as Arnoldus Montanus's Atlas Japannensis *(translated by John Ogilby in 1670). Combined together, they suggested a life devoted solely to the pursuit of pleasure.*

Witney Antiques

D2 Attributed to John Vanderbank (fl. 1689-1717)

D3 Attributed to Mary Holte (1684-1759)

Crewel work hanging. Coloured wools on a cotton and linen twill ground, the embroidered patterns with chinoiseries including a ho ho bird and a garden pavilion
279 x 235cm
English, c.1730-40

Probably cut from wall-hangings or bed-curtains, this embroidery in coloured worsteds (crewels) has been attributed to Mary Holte (1684-1759) of Aston Hall, Birmingham, on the basis of a hanging worked by Mary Holte and dated 1744. The hanging is supposed to have formed part of the furnishings at Aston Hall until 1775.

Birmingham Museums & Art Gallery, 1960 M.40.1

D4 Fan

Ivory, carved and painted guards, carved and painted sticks, vellum painted in watercolour and gouache
Length of guard 26.5cm
English, c.1755

The fan leaf is painted with a view based on Charles Grignion's (1721-1810) engraving after Canaletto of the Chinese pavilion at Ranelagh Gardens (see cat F8). The sticks have floral chinoiserie motifs in blue and gold.

The Fan Museum, London, HA 1000

D4 Fan

D5 Fan

Ivory, carved, pierced and painted with figures and flowers; paper fan leaf painted on both sides in watercolour, gold paint and coloured ink
Length of guard 29cm
Possibly French or German, c.1770s

The Chinese figures are in a style reminiscent of François Boucher (1703-1770). Gold foil, which was particularly favoured in Germany, has been applied to the mandarin figures.

The Fan Museum, London, HA 199

Main image: D12 Pair of shoes by Stead & Simpson, English, 1925
Victoria & Albert Museum

D6 Fan

Carved and pierced ivory, applied jasperware, vellum fan leaf with applied stipple engraved aquatint
Length of guard 27.5cm
English, c.1795-1800

The fan leaf is painted recto with figures which combine European, Chinese and Turkish features. The centre has a reserve coloured stipple engraving of the three Fine Arts (painting, architecture, sculpture) by Francesco Bartolozzi after Angelica Kauffman (1741-1807), 1780, published by Anthony Poggi, who commissioned drawings by Kauffman specifically for fans.

The Fan Museum, London, HA204

D6 Fan

D7 Fan

Red lacquer, vellum, watercolour and gold paint, mother-of-pearl, ivory
Length of guard 29cm
English, c.1800-1805

The fan leaf is elaborately painted and decorated in a chinoiserie style which is inspired by Chinese export wallpaper and painting. Some of the figures have costumes of applied mother-of-pearl with heads and necks of painted ivory.

The Fan Museum, London, HA974

D7 Fan (see main image, detail)

D8 Dragon robe

Red silk satin with embroidered dragons
104cm
Chinese, 19th century

Large numbers of dragon robes were acquired by western collectors after the declaration of the Chinese republic in 1911. The association of the dragon with the Chinese Emperor and the aura of romance of the Imperial Court appealed to westerners. Robes might be displayed in a variety of ways; fashionable western women might wear the robe at home, drape it over furniture, or even cut it up for its embroidered motifs. This example, altered and adapted for western use, started life as part of a bride's costume.

Royal Pavilion & Museums, Brighton & Hove, WA 505333

D9 Embroidery panel

Silk, embroidered
10.7 x 70.7cm
Chinese, late 18th century; mounted in the 20th century

Probably part of the sleeve of a mandarin's robe (see cat D8).

Royal Pavilion & Museums, Brighton & Hove, WA 505400

D10 Coat retailed by Liberty & Company

Black satin cut in kimono style and trimmed with Chinese floral embroidery
223cm (length)
English, c.1912

The mixture of motifs from Japan and China was typical of the time.

Royal Pavilion & Museums, Brighton & Hove, CT003630

D11 Pair of pyjamas

Blue satin with an embroidered dragon
107cm (length of trousers); 70cm (length of jacket)
French or English, 1920s

Royal Pavilion & Museums, Brighton & Hove, CTMAS000048

D11 Pair of pyjamas

D12 Pair of shoes by Stead & Simpson

Brown hand-painted satin with glued beads and a painted bird motif in blue and gold
13cm
English, 1925

The painted bird is clearly inspired by Chinese motifs.

Victoria & Albert Museum, T737B&C-1974

D13 Evening jacket by Mainbocher

Sequinned chinoiserie designs on a silk ground
55 x 40cm
French, 1939

Designed by Mainbocher, the first American couturier to open an outlet in Paris, this elegant chinoiserie jacket was worn by Lady Beit, a cousin of the Mitford sisters. It has the classic 1930s silhouette of a nipped-in waist and wide padded shoulders.

Victoria & Albert Museum, T309-1974

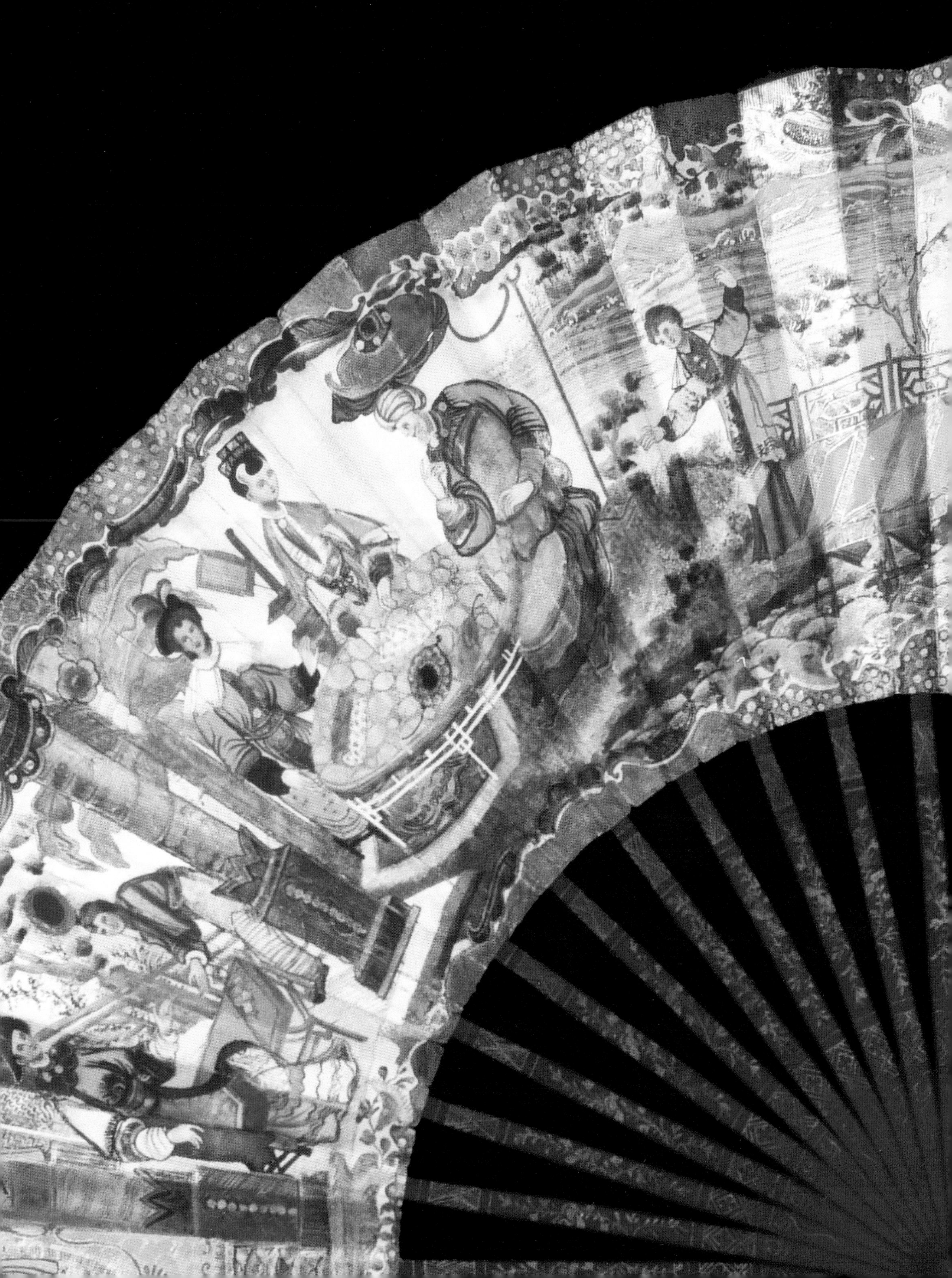

O D E

On the Death of a Favourite C A T,

Drowned in a Tub of Gold Fiſhes.

'TWAS on a lofty vaſe's ſide,
Where China's gayeſt art had dy'd
The azure flowers, that blow;
Demureſt of the tabby kind,
The penſive Selima reclin'd,
Gazed on the lake below.

Her conſcious tail her joy declar'd;
The fair round face, the ſnowy beard,
The velvet of her paws,
Her coat, that with the tortoiſe vies,
Her ears of jet, and emerald eyes,
She ſaw; and purr'd applauſe.

Still

Books

E1 Johan Nieuhof, ***An Embassy from the East India Company of the United Provinces to the Grand Tartar Cham Emperor of China*****, London 1669**

40.5cm

Nieuhof's Embassy *was first published in Dutch in 1665. Recording the Dutch embassy to China in 1655-7, it was the most comprehensive European record of Chinese life until the late 18th century. The English edition, translated by John Ogilby, contains 113 plates copied by Wenceslaus Hollar and Francis Place from the originals after Nieuhof. Nieuhof wrote 'All things necessary for the sustenance of Man, as well as for his delight, are to be had [in China]'. The book was a major source for chinoiserie.*

Victoria & Albert Museum, L510-1926

E2 George Parker, ***A Treatise of Japaning and Varnishing...*****, London, 1688**

38cm

This is an extremely rare copy of the famous pattern book better known as Stalker and Parker's Treatise. Four editions were published in 1688, in one of which George Parker 'varnisher and japaner' (sic) appears as the sole author. This copy boasts a 'japanned' cover presumably by Parker (see cat E3).

Evan Bedford Library of Furniture History

E3 John Stalker, ***A Treatise of Japaning and Varnishing together with Above an Hundred distinct Patterns for Japan work, in Imitation of the Indians...*****, London, 1688**

38cm

This is a working copy of Stalker and Parker's famous Treatise. *One of the earliest chinoiserie pattern books, it provided designs and recipes for decorating furniture to resemble true oriental lacquer. The 'oriental' designs, some of which derive from Nieuhof (see cat E1), were on the authors' own admission 'helpt a little' when they were 'lame'. Motifs were derived from imported lacquer, porcelain, engravings and patterned silks, though few of the authors' chinoiseries appear on extant pieces.*

John Hardy

E4 Jean-Baptiste Du Halde, ***A Description of the Empire of China...*****, London, 1741**

42cm

Du Halde's Description *was first published in France in 1735. The author, a Jesuit priest, never visited China, and the work is partly based on previous Jesuit accounts. It remained influential throughout the 18th century. The book is open at a plate showing the astronomical observatory at Peking (Beijing), which can still be seen.*

Rare Books & Special Collections,
Jubilee Library, Brighton, F915.1

E5 William Halfpenny, ***Twenty New Designs of Chinese Lattice...*****, London, 1750**

30.5cm

Only one edition of this rare series of chinoiserie designs was published. The book's title comes from a contemporary advertisement as no title page is known.

Evan Bedford Library of Furniture History

E6 ***Designs by Mr. R. Bentley for Six Poems by Mr. T. Gray*****, London, 1753**

Engravings by Johann Sebastian Muller (1715- c.1792) and Charles Grignion (1721-1810) after Richard Bentley (1708-1782)

30cm

This famous book, sponsored by Horace Walpole, is open at the 'Ode on the Death of a Favourite Cat'. Walpole himself provided an explanatory text in which he refers to 'a Mandarine-Cat sitting before a Chinese pagoda, and angling for a gold (fish) into a china jar; and another cat drawing up a net. At the bottom are mice enjoying themselves on the prospect of the cat's death.' The etching, by Muller, is a delightfully whimsical example of rococo chinoiserie (see also cat F11).

Victoria & Albert Museum, 3-8041-800

Main image: E6 *Designs by Mr. R. Bentley for Six Poems by Mr. T. Gray*, London, 1753, Victoria & Albert Museum

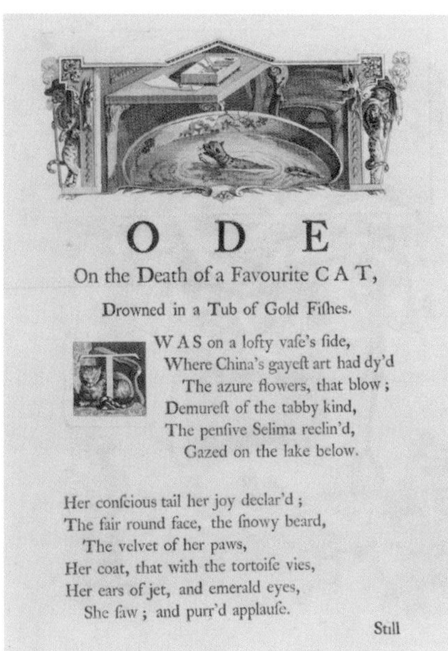

ODE

On the Death of a Favourite CAT,

Drowned in a Tub of Gold Fiſhes.

TWAS on a lofty vaſe's ſide,
Where China's gayeſt art had dy'd
The azure flowers, that blow;
Demureſt of the tabby kind,
The penſive Selima reclin'd,
Gazed on the lake below.

Her conſcious tail her joy declar'd;
The fair round face, the ſnowy beard,
The velvet of her paws,
Her coat, that with the tortoiſe vies,
Her ears of jet, and emerald eyes,
She ſaw; and purr'd applauſe.

Still

E6 *Designs by Mr. R. Bentley for Six Poems by Mr. T. Gray*, London, 1753

E7 William and John Halfpenny, *Rural Architecture in the Chinese Taste*, 3rd ed. London, 1755

22cm

First published in 1750 under a different title, the book is of particular interest for its depiction of rococo-Chinese furniture and chimneypieces. William Halfpenny produced the earliest pattern books of chinoiserie garden buildings.

Evan Bedford Library of Furniture History

E8 William Chambers, *Designs of Chinese Buildings, Furniture, Dresses, Machines and Utensils...* London, 1757

51cm

The architect William Chambers (1723-1796) made three voyages to the East from 1740-1749 visiting Canton at least twice, but not inland China from which European merchants were excluded. Here he studied Chinese design at first-hand. His book was intended to put a stop to 'the extravagancies that daily appear under the name of Chinese'. The engravings, however, accord with classical principles of design and even include European decorative details; some of the designs appear to be of the author's own devising. The book, however, was the first serious attempt to record the architecture of China and was to be extremely influential throughout Europe after c1770. Both the Chinese room at Carlton House and the interiors of the Royal Pavilion in Brighton owe much to Chambers's designs.

Rare Books & Special Collections, Jubilee Library, Brighton, F720.951 CHA

E9 Charles Over, *Ornamental Architecture in the Gothic, Chinese and Modern Taste...* London, 1758

22cm

Over followed the Halfpennys' lead in providing designs for Chinese buildings intended 'for gardens, parks, forests, woods, canals etc.'

Rare Books & Special Collections, Jubilee Library, Brighton

E10 P Decker, *Chinese Architecture Civil and Ornamental*, London, 1759

23cm

'Paul Decker', if he existed at all, plagiarised 21 of the 24 designs from Edwards and Darly's A New Book of Chinese Designs *... (1754). Illustrations range from an 'Imperial Retreat' to 'The Summer Dwelling of a Chief Bonza or Priest.'*

Evan Bedford Library of Furniture History

E11 *The Ladies Amusement; or, whole Art of Japaning Made Easy...* London, c.1762

20.3cm

This extremely rare, possibly unique, edition contains over 1,500 hand-coloured engravings by Jean Pillement and others intended as designs to decorate porcelain, silver, lacquer, enamels etc. It was issued in at least two editions from 1758-1762.

Evan Bedford Library of Furniture History

E12 William Chambers, *Plans, Elevations, Sections ... of the Gardens and Buildings at Kew in Surrey*, London 1763

55cm

Chambers is best-known for the pagoda at Kew Gardens, which he designed as part of an extensive remodelling of the garden for the royal family. Inspired by the famous 'porcelain' pagoda at Nanking (Nanjing), depicted in Nieuhof's Embassy, the Kew pagoda was built in 1761-2 and must have been a striking sight for originally it was covered with plates of varnished iron of different colours and the roof angles were adorned with 80 dragons. The building established Chambers's reputation as an authority on Chinese buildings, though it was never meant to be archaeologically correct. Horace Walpole wrote in 1761 'We begin to perceive the Tower at Kew from Montpelier Row; in a fortnight you will see it in Yorkshire'.

Rare Books & Special Collections, Jubilee Library, Brighton, F728.3 CHA

E14 Thomas Sheraton, *The Cabinet Maker and Upholsterer's Drawing Book and Repository*, London, 1793

E13 Mathias Lock and H Copland, *A New Book of Ornaments consisting of Tables, Chimnies, Sconces, Spandles, Clock Cases, Candle Stands...* 2nd ed. 1768

35.5cm

Chinoiserie motifs appeared in the first edition (1752) and are repeated here. Lock and Copland were early pioneers in publishing ornament in the rococo or 'French' taste.

Victoria & Albert Museum, E5035-5046-1907

E14 Thomas Sheraton, *The Cabinet Maker and Upholsterer's Drawing Book and Repository*, London, 1793

26.2cm

Sheraton's famous pattern book contains the only known views of the Chinese Drawing Room at Carlton House, designed in c.1787-90 by Henry Holland and Dominique Daguerre for George, Prince of Wales. George almost single-handedly revived the flagging taste for chinoiserie, though many of the decorative details derive from William Chambers's Design of Chinese Buildings*... (1757). Sheraton's two views are dated 6 October and 1 November 1793. In 1819 the majority of the contents were sent to the Royal Pavilion.*

Leeds Museums & Galleries (Temple Newsam)

E15 Sir George Staunton, *An Authentic Account of an Embassy from the King of Great Britain to the Emperor of China*, London, 1797

59cm

The aim of Earl Macartney's embassy (1792-4) was the establishment of sovereign equality between King George III and the Qianlong Emperor together with improved trading conditions in Canton and a permanent British mission in Peking (Beijing). Diplomatically it was a failure, but the embassy gathered much useful information about China and the drawings by William Alexander, which accompanied the text, remained the major source for 'authentic' portrayals of China for 50 years. They provided the impetus for a spectacular late flowering of chinoiserie in the early 19th century. A separate book of plates was issued with the text.

Rare Books & Special Collections, Jubilee Library, Brighton, 915.1 STA

E16 William Alexander, *Picturesque Representations of the Dress and Manners of the Chinese*, 1814

William Alexander (1767-1816) was draughtsman to the embassy to China led by Lord Macartney (see cat E15). His drawings of China influenced both Henry Holland's and William Porden's unexecuted schemes for re-modelling the Pavilion in a Chinese style (see cat F24, F26). The Picturesque Representations is Alexander's last published work.

Rare Books & Special Collections, Jubilee Library, Brighton, 391 AL2

Pictures, Prints and Drawings, and Wallpaper

F1 Osias Beert (c.1580-1623)

Still Life with Nautilus Cup, Fruit, Nuts and Wine, c.1610
Oil on panel
56.3 x 75.8cm

At the beginning of the 17th century the Dutch took over the near monopoly of eastern trade from the Portuguese and imported large amounts of Chinese porcelain to Europe. The Wanli (1573-1619) bowl amongst the arrangement of delicacies and precious things illustrates the prestige attached to Chinese porcelain at this date.

Royal Pavilion & Museums, Brighton & Hove, FA000061

F1 Osias Beert (c.1580-1623)

F2 After Johan Nieuhof (1618-1672)

Triumphal Arch, c.1669
Engraving
10.5 x 15cm

Nieuhof's Embassy *(see cat EI) contained 113 plates based on sketches made in China by Nieuhof. In the two English editions the original plates were copied by Wenceslaus Hollar and Francis Place.*

Stephen Calloway

F3 Attributed to Robert Robinson (?1651-1706)

Chinoiserie painted panel, c.1696
Oil on panel
205 x 79cm

This panel forms part of a scheme attributed to the engraver, publisher, and scenery designer Robinson on the basis of a signed panel at the Sir John Cass Schools, Aldgate, London. Robinson's fabulously exotic world was probably inspired by prints after Nieuhof's Embassy *as well as Chinese exports. Robinson's chinoiserie wall paintings are some of the earliest known.*

Victoria & Albert Museum, P9-1954

F4 Michel Aubert (c.1700-1757) after Antoine Watteau (1684-1721)

Idole de la Déesse Ki Mâo Sâo dans le Royaume de Mang au pays de Laos c.1730
Engraving
32 x 39.5cm

Around 1710 Watteau was commissioned to decorate the Cabinet du Roi in the Château de la Muette, a hunting lodge outside Paris. This very early chinoiserie scheme only survived until 1741, but prints were made by Aubert and others. It is possible Watteau had access to Chinese prints as Mâo Sâo may be a corruption of Miáo Shan, a manifestation of Kuan Yin, goddess of mercy, or Mazu, goddess of the oceans, one of the few names of Chinese deities familiar to westerners. The goddess has been likened to a Parisian courtesan holding a parasol and a feather duster.

Private collection

F3 Attributed to Robert Robinson (?1651-1706)

Main image: F14 Thomas Robins
The Park at Honington Hall, Warwickshire, 1759
Mr and Mrs Stephen Clark

F4 Michel Aubert (c.1700-1757) after Antoine Watteau (1684-1721)

F5 Robert le Vrac de Tournières (1668-1752)
Portrait of Richard Bateman, 1741
Oil on canvas
49 x 35.8cm

Richard 'Dickie' Bateman, remodelled the gardens at Grove House, Old Windsor, Berkshire, between 1730-1741. Chinese features appeared on the estate in 1735. Here Bateman wears a Chinese embroidered gown, points to a Chinese scroll, and, behind, is a Chinese porch. Bateman's house was described as 'half gothic, half attick, half Chinese, and completely fribble'.

Birmingham Museums & Art Gallery, P19,1974

F5 Robert le Vrac de Tournières (1668-1752)

F6 William Hogarth (1697-1764)
Marriage à la Mode: The Tête à Tête, c.1743
Oil on canvas
70 x 90.8cm

The collection of blanc de chine porcelain on the chimneypiece and the chinoiserie clock accord with the theme of sexual transgression implicit and explicit in Hogarth's morality tale (see p.23). Hogarth is making a clear link between Viscountess Squanderfield's taste for Chinese porcelain and her failed marriage.

National Gallery, London, bought 1824, NG114

F6 William Hogarth (1697-1764)

F7 Trade Card of Benjamin Clitherow, Fireworker, c.1750
Etching and engraving
33.1 x 20.3cm

A fantastic rococo confection with, appropriately, Chinese lattice railing. Fireworks include 'China fire'.

The Trustees of the British Museum, D2-2276 Banks

F8 Charles Grignion (1721-1810) after Antonio Canaletto (1697-1768)
A View of the Canal, Chinese Building, Rotondo etc in Ranelagh Gardens after the Masquerade, 1751
Etching and engraving
26 x 40cm

Ranelagh Gardens, Chelsea, opened in 1742 as a rival to Vauxhall. Chinoiserie buildings, thought particularly appropriate for pleasure gardens, soon appeared including this whimsical structure, erected in 1750. It was intended for masquerade parties.

The Trustees of the British Museum, 1880-11-13-2450

F9 Thomas Bowles (fl. 1712-1753) after Samuel Wale (died 1786)
A View of the Chinese Pavilions and Boxes in Vauxhall Gardens, 1751; this impression 1830s
Engraving
28.7 x 41.8cm

There is little that is recognisably Chinese in the so-called Chinese pavilions added to the Vauxhall Pleasure Gardens in about 1750-51. The fact that they were called Chinese illustrates the contemporary confusion between Chinese and gothic. The ceiling of the middle pavilion was painted in the 'Chinese manner', although the subject was Vulcan catching Mars and Venus.

The Trustees of the British Museum, 1875,0508.1456

F10 J Haynes (fl. 1730-1753)
A View of the Mandarine Yacht and Belvedere ... Virginia Water, 1753
Etching
9.2 x 28.7cm

The 'Mandarine' yacht was created from an existing boat in 1753 for the Duke of Cumberland, younger son of George II. Possibly designed by Henry Flitcroft, it must have been wonderfully exotic with its winged dragon decorating the hull and the central pavilion which functioned as a Great Room for entertaining.

The Royal Collection, RCIN 700787

F10 J Haynes (fl. 1730-1753)

F11 Johan Sebastian Müller (c.1715-92) after Richard Bentley (1708-82)

Headpiece to Designs by Mr. R. Bentley for Six Poems by Mr. T. Gray, 1753
Etching
7 x 17cm

Thomas Gray's 'Ode on the Death of a Favourite Cat' (1747) recounts the story of the demise of Horace Walpole's cat 'pensive Selima'. The headpiece to the poem has two cat pallbearers who frame the cat's last moments (see cat E6).

Stephen Calloway

F12 Thomas Chippendale (1718-1779)

Three Chinese Chairs, 1753
Pen and grey wash
20.4 x 34cm

No fewer than 64 plates of the first edition of Chippendale's Gentleman and Cabinet Maker's Director *(1754) exhibit chinoiserie characteristics. He was particularly proud of his nine lattice-back chairs, hoping that they would improve a taste which 'yet never arrived to any perfection'. Motifs were adapted from Matthew Darley's* A New Book of Chinese, Gothic and Modern Chairs *(1751) as well as from Chinese export wallpapers. This drawing was engraved by Matthew Darly for pl. XXIV of the first edition of the* Director *and pl. XXVI of the third edition of 1762.*

The Chippendale Society, C1975/4a

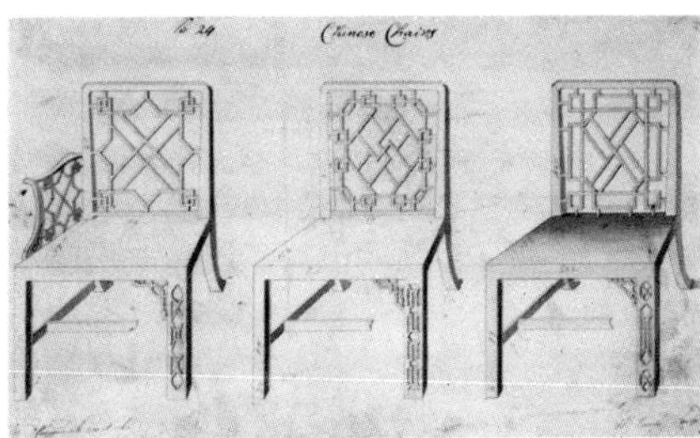

F12 Thomas Chippendale (1718-1779)

F13 Paul Sandby (1730-1809) and Thomas Sandby (1721/3-1798)

Virginia Water from the Manor Lodge, c.1754
Watercolour
43 x 76.3cm

On a crowded shore, the Duke of Cumberland shows his 'Mandarine' yacht (cat F10) to a crowd of onlookers.

The Royal Collection, RL14646

F13 Paul Sandby (1730-1809) and Thomas Sandby (1721/3-1798)

F14 Thomas Robins (1716-1770)

The Park at Honington Hall, Warwickshire, 1759
Pen, ink and watercolour
33 x 49cm

The park at Honington Hall was laid out by Sanderson Miller c.1753-60. Robins's view shows the Chinese pavilion overlooking the River Stour and a Chinese bridge with 'double braced' Chinese paling. The picture is framed by a garland of English wild flowers.

Mr and Mrs Stephen Clark

F14 Thomas Robins (1716-1770)

F15 John Fougeron (fl. 1761-70)

Trade card of Domenico Negri, Confectioner, c1760-65
Etching and engraving
16.2 x 19cm

Negri's trade card is a lively example of rococo chinoiserie. Negri was a well-known confectioner trading from 'the Pineapple' in Berkeley Square, London.

The Trustees of the British Museum, Heal 48.43

F16 Chinoiserie figure group wallpaper, c.1760

Hand block-printed in distemper
148 x 122cm
English

This extremely rare rococo chinoiserie paper was found beneath panelling in a house in Banbury, Oxfordshire. It is of unusually large size and has been incorrectly aligned so that the intended asymmetrical effect has been lost. Instead of standing on a horizontal axis, the figures were intended to be seen diagonally.

The Whitworth Art Gallery, University of Manchester, W1995.6

F17 Charles Grignion (1721-1810) after Thomas Sandby (1721-1798)

A View of the Menagerie and its Pavilion … at Kew, 1763
Etching
30.5 x 46.4cm

The plate is from William Chambers's Plans, elevations, sections … of the gardens and buildings at Kew *(1763). The menagerie or pheasant ground at Kew was designed by Chambers in 1760. The light insubstantial nature of Chinese architecture was well suited to menageries (which housed birds as much as animals). Appropriately enough, the Kew menagerie contained 'great numbers of Chinese and Tartarian pheasants'.*

The Trustees of the British Museum, 1863,0509.278

F18 Man and boy wallpaper, c.1770

Intaglio printed with engraved metal plates; colours applied in watercolour, possibly through a stencil.
98.5 x 78cm
English

See cat F19

The Whitworth Art Gallery, University of Manchester, W1967.281.3

F19 Goose and dragon wallpaper, c. 1770

Intaglio printed with engraved metal plates; colours applied in watercolour, possibly through a stencil.
98.5 x 78cm
English

Hand-painted Chinese papers were extremely expensive, and to satisfy demand English manufacturers produced chinoiserie papers from the early 18th century. This example imitates motifs from Chinese export wallpaper and porcelain.

The Whitworth Art Gallery, University of Manchester, W1967.281.3

F20 Sparrow (fl. 1770s)

The Prospect of the Porcelane Tower at Nan Kong in China, 1778
Engraving
23.2 x 36.6cm

Engraved for John Hamilton Moore's A New and Complete Collection of Voyages and Travels, *1778, the so-called porcelain tower of Nanking (Nanjing) was, thanks to its appearance in Nieuhof's Embassy, the best-known Chinese building in Europe. Built in 1412-1441 and destroyed in 1856, the pagoda was faced with green, red and yellow tiles.*

Patrick Conner

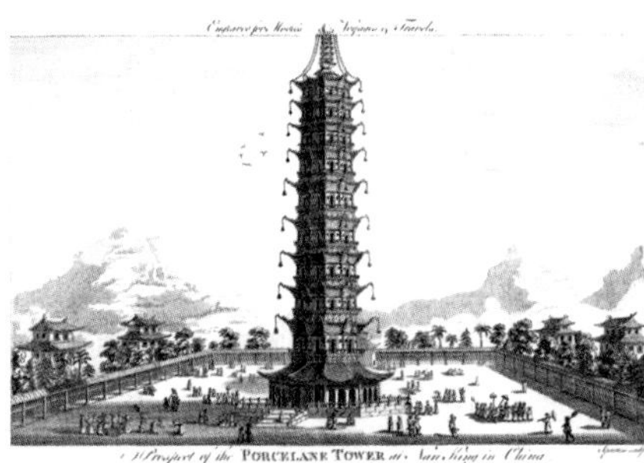

F20 Sparrow (fl. 1770s)

F21 James Gillray (1756-1815)

The Reception of the Diplomatique and his Suite at the Court of Pekin, 1792
Etching
31 x 40cm

The print depicts the embassy of Lord Macartney to the Qianlong Emperor of China. The embassy's aim was to open trade to China and permit a permanent mission to Peking (Beijing). Gillray depicts the emperor contemptuously dismissing Macartney's diplomatic gifts: 'I set no value on objects strange or ingenious, and have no use for your country's manufactures'. What is extraordinary is that Gillray has virtually predicted the diplomatic failure of the embassy as the print was published before the embassy reached Peking.

Royal Pavilion & Museums, Brighton & Hove, FA208426

F22 Bird and flower wallpaper, c.1790-1800

Hand-painted in ink, gouache and distemper colours on a green ground
317 x 92cm
Chinese

This paper, which may have been supplied by Robson and Hale to the Royal Pavilion in 1815, is of the 'bird and flower' type, where a flowering tree climbs the length of the paper from rocks at the base. Papers of this type were made for export; they were not used in China. Chinese craftsmen developed the papers from two native traditions: painted silk hangings used as wall decorations, and plain paper stuck to the wall. Chinese export wallpaper (often known as 'India' paper because it was imported by the East India Company), was always expensive and was usually mounted on canvas on battens; each length of paper was made of smaller sheets pasted together. It was considered appropriate for intimate domestic spaces, often associated with women: bedrooms, dressing rooms and, less usually, drawing rooms.

Royal Pavilion & Museums, Brighton & Hove

F21 James Gillray (1756-1815)

F23 William Alexander (1767-1816)

A Chinese Comic Actor, c.1793
Pen, pencil and watercolour
22.2 x 18.4cm

Alexander was draughtsman to the British embassy to China 1792-4. This figure represents an enraged military officer; it inspired the design for the central panel of the window of the north staircase at the Royal Pavilion. The figure was reproduced in Alexander's Costume of China *(1805).*

Royal Pavilion & Museums, Brighton & Hove, FA100048

F24 William Porden (1755-1822)

Design for the Royal Pavilion in the Chinese style, c.1805
Pen, ink and watercolour
58 x 107.5cm

The disparity in scale between the existing Marine Pavilion and the new stables led George, Prince of Wales, to commission a Chinese design from William Porden. Porden's three designs reflect the proportions and the colour of Chinese buildings depicted by William Alexander (see cat E15), although the hexagonal turret looks back to 18th century chinoiserie.

Royal Pavilion & Museums, Brighton & Hove, FA101340

F25 William Porden (1755-1822)

Design for the North Front of the Royal Pavilion in the Chinese style, c.1805
Pen, ink and watercolour
62 x 111cm

Exhibited at the Royal Academy in 1806, this design is, like cat F26, an adaptation of Henry Holland's existing building. Porden has here included Chinese characters beneath the entrance canopies and life-size Chinese figures in niches.

Royal Pavilion & Museums, Brighton & Hove, FA101339

F26 William Porden (1755 – 1822)

Design for the East Front of the Royal Pavilion in the Chinese style, c.1805
Pen, ink and watercolour
61.5 X 110.5cm

In this design Porden has embellished the existing Marine Pavilion with bright red columns, gilded dragons, and a roof of grey-blue tiles. Motifs may have been taken from the Qianlong Emperor's summer palace as depicted by William Alexander. The design has no fewer than six different lattice patterns and 12 different friezes.

Royal Pavilion & Museums, Brighton & Hove, FA101338

F27 Gaetano Landi (fl. 1810)

Chinese Drawing Room, 1810
Aquatint
24 x 34cm

Landi's 'Sino-Piranesian' fantasy introduces what has been called 'a hot Latin note' to Regency design. The room is full of spatial ambiguities and fantastic decoration more extravagant than the post 1815 interiors of the Royal Pavilion. Although described as a drawing room, it is possible that Landi intended a lavish garden pavilion. The print was published in 1810 in Landi's Architectural Decorations.

Patrick Conner

F28 M Dubourg after J H Clark (c.1770-1863)

The Chinese Bridge and Pagoda Erected in the Park..., 1814
Aquatint
17 x 22.2cm

A year before his oriental experiments at the Royal Pavilion in Brighton, the architect John Nash built a bridge and pagoda in St James's Park as a framework for a lavish firework display which formed part of the Grand

F30 Augustus Charles Pugin (1767/8-1832)

National Jubilee celebration of the centenary of the Hanoverian dynasty. The pagoda sadly burned and collapsed.

Royal Pavilion & Museums, Brighton & Hove, FATMP001340

F29 After Frederick Crace (1779-1859)

Design for a ho ho bird, c.1815
Pen, ink and watercolour
29 x 23cm

The design is inscribed 'The Royal Bird Foo hum', which may be a corruption of feng and huang (pheasant and peacock). Fum was also the caricaturist's name for King George IV. The phoenix or ho ho bird, a bird of good omen, was a favourite Crace motif. In this instance, the design may have been intended for the Yellow Drawing Room in the Royal Pavilion.

Royal Pavilion & Museums, Brighton & Hove, FA100445

F30 Augustus Charles Pugin (1767/8-1832)

The Yellow Drawing Room, Royal Pavilion, c.1815-20
Pencil and watercolour
20.5 x 29.8cm

The Yellow Drawing Room, now the Music Room Gallery, was remodelled and redecorated in 1815 by Frederick Crace, though Robert Jones may also have been employed. Chinese export paintings were placed on the walls and the room was enriched with carved dragons and exotic birds. The scheme was replaced in 1821 but, while it lasted, it represented the apogee of revived rococo chinoiserie.

Royal Pavilion & Museums, Brighton & Hove, FA100698

F31 George, Prince of Wales, later George IV (1762-1830)

Design for the bamboo cove and a wall panel of the Music Room of the Royal Pavilion, 1818
Pencil
22.6 x 18.2cm

Built by John Nash in 1815-1817, the Music Room was decorated by Frederick Crace under the direction of George, Prince of Wales. According to an inscription on this sketch, this design was drawn by the Prince Regent in 1818 'when I (Frederick Crace) had the honour of attending HRH to receive his commands … (this) being the first idea for the ornaments forming the panels of the New Music Room.' There is another design on verso.

The Trustees of the British Museum, 1962,0714.34

F32 Augustus Charles Pugin (1767/8 – 1832)

The Long Gallery, Royal Pavilion, c.1819
Pencil and watercolour
21 x 30cm

The Long Gallery was created by John Nash in 1815. The walls were covered with canvas painted with bamboo and life-size Chinese figures were supplied by Crace. Notable here are the splendid standards with lanterns supplied by Fricker and Henderson.

Royal Pavilion & Museums, Brighton & Hove, FA100692

F33 After Frederick Crace (1779-1859)

Design for a lantern and standard, c.1815
Pen, ink and watercolour
32 x 23cm

The Crace ledgers for 1815 record that 16 carved standards were supplied by Fricker and Henderson for the Long Gallery of the Royal Pavilion. The ultimate source for the standards may be an engraved view in Johan Nieuhof's Embassy *(see cat E1) of a street in Nanking (Nanjing) with tradesmen's standards in the form of pennants attached to poles.*

Royal Pavilion & Museums, Brighton & Hove, FA100433

F34 After Frederick Crace (1779-1859)

Design for a Skylight, c.1815
Pen, ink and watercolour
28 x 2cm

This design is for the south staircase skylight. The splendid dragon is much more like a Chinese dragon than most of the Europeanised dragons in the Royal Pavilion. The bats in the corners of the design were regarded as creatures of good omen in Chinese art.

Royal Pavilion & Museums, Brighton & Hove, FA100381

F35 Anonymous

By Royal Authority: A New Way of mounting your Horse in Spite of the Gout, c.1816
Etching
22.2 x 34.6cm

Chinoiserie is here used to satirise the gout-afflicted king. George IV, absurdly over-dressed, is lowered onto his horse in front of a chinoiserie pavilion. Mandarin figures provide a wedge to prevent the chair rolling backwards and the pagoda in the background, usually evocative of Kew, here represents a generalised exoticism.

Royal Pavilion & Museums, Brighton & Hove, FA200657

F36 Attributed to William Heath (1795-1840)

New Baubles for the Chinese Temple, 1820
Etching
22.2 x 31.5cm

George IV demands money commensurate with his new status as king. It is clear that he intends to spend it on the extravagant chinoiserie interior of the Royal Pavilion, evoked by mandarins, a pagod and a pagoda.

Royal Pavilion & Museums, Brighton & Hove, FA200652

F37 Attributed to William Heath (1795-1840)

Baise-Mon-Q, 1820
Etching
34.5 x 24.3cm

The 'Q' of the title was the wife of Colonel George Quentin of the 10th Hussars, with whom the king was alleged to be having an affair. Chinoiserie is once again used to satirise the king's excesses; a drawing of the Pavilion is entitled 'The Palace of Fum' and the obese mandarin balancing on the head of a dragon is 'The Great Fum'. 'Fum' was a name frequently given to the king as an allusion to his oriental tastes (see cat F29).

Royal Pavilion & Museums, Brighton & Hove, FA207992

F38 John Buonarotti Papworth (1775-1847)

Design for F & R Sparrow's Tea Warehouse (right) and sketch elevation of the façade (left), 1822
Sepia pen with sepia, blue and yellow washes with pencil
59 x 43.5cm

Papworth's design for a tea warehouse at Ludgate Hill, London, may well be the first urban building to possess a Chinese façade. It boasts lei-wen spirals, urns and bells, and a Chinese figure in a niche.

RIBA Library Drawings and Archives Collections, PB1305/PAP/88

F39 William Daniell (1769-1837)

The Boat House, Fishing Temple and Tents from the South Bank of Virginia Water, 1827
Pencil and watercolour
33 x 51cm

Daniell's view shows Wyatville's orginal design for the Fishing Temple (see cat F42) before Frederick Crace's alterations in 1827.

Royal Pavilion & Museums, Brighton & Hove, FA103650

F39 William Daniell (1769-1837)

F40 William Daniell (1769-1837)

The Boat House, Fishing Temple and Tents from the South Bank of Virginia Water, c.1829
Aquatint
28 x 48cm

The print shows the changes made to the Fishing Temple by Frederick Crace in 1827. According to the Morning Chronicle *of 8 December 1827 the king himself took a considerable part in the design of his 'other pavilion' (see cat F42). Interestingly, the later alterations harked back to William Chambers and mid-18th century rococo chinoiserie rather than to William Alexander. The exoticism is increased by the presence of 'Turkish' tents and a 'Chinese' boat house.*

Royal Pavilion & Museums, Brighton & Hove, FA207916

F41 Robert Seymour (1798-1836)

The Great Joss and His Playthings, 1829
Etching
22.4 x 33.1cm

A masterly satire on King George IV's love of chinoiserie and wasteful excess. The king is portrayed as a joss or idol; the pose recalls images of Budai, the Chinese god of happiness. Here he sits on the treasury teapot, which spouts sovereigns to pay for his projects. The 'C' formed by the king's hookah is a reference to his mistress, Lady Conyngham.

Royal Pavilion & Museums, Brighton & Hove, FA200654

F42 William Delamotte (1775-1863)

The North Front of the Fishing Temple, Virginia Water, c.1829
Watercolour
15 x 19.5cm

A miniature Brighton Pavilion for the pleasure of George IV, the Fishing Temple was designed by the king and his architect, Jeffry Wyatville, in 1825. Two years later Frederick Crace designed the interior, which must have resembled his schemes for the Royal Pavilion. Crace also heightened the roof and added more oriental detail. Fishing – simple, passive and unwarlike – had long been associated with western fantasies of China and the chinoiserie style of the king's 'Temple' was an appropriate choice.

The Royal Collection, RL17512

F42 William Delamotte (1775-1863)

F43 William Delamotte (1775-1863)

The Building on China Island, Virginia Water, c.1829-1836
Pencil
15 x 19.5cm

The Chinese Building on China Island was built in 1757-8 as a tea house for the Duke of Cumberland. The architect may have been Thomas Anson, who served with the duke and built the Chinese House at Shugborough in c.1747. The exterior was brightly painted and decorated with bells and Chinese ornaments. Three 'umbrellas' surmounted the three principal elements of the composition. The central 'Great Room' boasted chairs 'carved, painted and part gilt in Chinese taste'.

The Royal Collection, RL17509

F43 William Delamotte (1775-1863)

F44 Samuel Sanders Teulon (1812-1878)

Design for the Chinese Fishing Temple at Virginia Water, 1860
Pen, ink and watercolour
43 x 61.5cm

In 1860 Prince Albert commissioned Teulon to repair Wyatville's Fishing Temple (see cat F42). In addition to the repairs, Teulon made a detailed drawing to show 'the style of decoration purposed for the entire exterior.' He evidently hoped to restore Frederick Crace's colour scheme of the 1830s. This work was not carried out and the building was demolished and replaced in 1867.

RIBA Library, Drawings and Archives Collections, PB107/1

F44 Samuel Sanders Teulon (1812-1878)

F45 Arthur Elsley (1861-1952)

Faithful and Fearless: Portrait of Kylin, c.1920
Oil on canvas
45 x 54cm

Kylin (1909-1924) was the favourite pet of Ellen Thomas-Stanford of Preston Manor, Brighton. Ellen believed her dog to be a Pekingese and she named it after her collection of Buddhist lions, which she mistakenly called 'kylins' after the mythical Chinese qilin. From about 1900 a select group of women were breeding Pekingese dogs and by the 1920s they were the height of fashion. It was thought that the dogs had a semi-sacred status in China and that when bred in Britain (and Kylin is a very British peke) they retained a 'memory' of China. Pekingese dogs are part of 20th century chinoiserie.

Royal Pavilion & Museums, Brighton & Hove, FAPM090065

F46 Richard Jack (1866 -1952)

The Chinese Chippendale Drawing Room at Buckingham Palace, 1926
Oil on canvas
101.7 x 127cm

Queen Mary and Sir Charles Allom of White Allom & Co created the Chinese Chippendale Room in 1911. The queen was a connoisseur and collector (especially of jade) and she furnished her drawing room with Chinese and chinoiserie objects, some of which had originally been in the Royal Pavilion in Brighton. Wallpaper was specially printed using a pattern from Chinese silk and furniture was covered with 'mandarin' robes.

The Royal Collection. RCIN 405848

F47 George Barbier (1882 -1932)

La Paresse (Sloth), 1925
Stencilled print
25.2 x 16.2cm

From a set of prints of the Seven Deadly Sins produced in a portfolio entitled 'Frills and

F46 Richard Jack (1866 -1952)

Curlicues'. Two women lounge on cushions in an oriental interior; one has fallen asleep while reading Proust, the other blows smoke rings from a cigarette. The air of decadence and sexual ambiguity is heightened by their quasi-male Chinese pyjama suits and short hair.

Royal Pavilion & Museums, Brighton & Hove,

F48 Cathay Decoration wallpaper, c.1927
Hand printed and stencilled
133 x 53cm
Designed by Heffer, Scott and Company; manufactured by John Line & Sons

Part of John Line's 'Distinctive Decorations' range, the paper, the manufacturer claimed, could be used with any other type of furnishing and boasted 'brilliant colouring and refined drawing'. The pattern of trees, flowers and pagodas was intended to start above the skirting board; it could be adjusted to suit the architectural features of the room.

The Whitworth Art Gallery, University of Manchester, W1987.269.2

F49 Festival of Lanterns wallpaper, c.1930
Hand-stencilled and embossed
162cm (length)
Designed by W W Clarke Pitts or studio (1881-1936); manufactured by John Line & Sons

Printed in the brilliant colours of the jazz era, this frieze paper owes more to Hollywood than the East. It evokes the romanticised orient of the world of Chu Chin Chow, a pseudo-Chinese musical which opened in 1916 and ran for nearly five years. The Journal of Decorative Art *suggested that it would make an ideal café decoration.*

The Whitworth Art Gallery, University of Manchester, W1972.16

F50 Kaiwan wallpaper, c.1950-55
Hand-printed with silkscreens
90 x 40cm (open)
Manufactured by John Line

Contained in a pattern book, Kaiwan was available in two colourways. Displayed here is the version with a turquoise ground tipped in gold. The pattern was described as 'late 18th century chinoiserie'.

The Whitworth Art Gallery, University of Manchester, W1987.276.6

Contributors to the Catalogue

STELLA BEDDOE. Senior Keeper and Keeper of Decorative Art, Royal Pavilion & Museums, Brighton & Hove. She has published widely on the decorative arts, particularly ceramics, from English earthenwares to Art Deco and Fairies in literature and the visual arts.

DAVID BEEVERS. Keeper of Fine Art, Royal Pavilion & Museums, Brighton & Hove. Formerly Keeper of Preston Manor, he has published on many aspects of the fine and decorative arts.

SARAH CHEANG. Senior Lecturer in Cultural and Historical Studies, London College of Fashion. Her research has focussed on the reception of Chinese material culture in Britain in the 19th and 20th centuries. Dr Cheang's most recent publications include a study of the uses of Chinese embroideries in British homes, and a history of the Pekingese dog in Britain.

PATRICK CONNER. Director, Martyn Gregory Gallery, London, specialists in historical paintings related to China and its relations with Europe. From 1975 to 1986 he was Keeper of Fine Art at the Royal Pavilion, Art Gallery & Museums, Brighton. In 1986 he organised the exhibition *The China Trade 1600–1860*. Dr Conner is the author of *Oriental Architecture in the West* (London, 1979).

JAMES LOMAX. Curator of Collections at Temple Newsam (Leeds Museums & Galleries). He has published extensively on various aspects of the fine and decorative arts and curated numerous exhibitions especially on silver. He is a former Chairman of the Silver Society and is Honorary Curator of the Chippendale Society.

C5 Cabinet on stand, English, c.1690-1700
The Holburne Museum of Art, Bath

Copyright Credits

The Royal Collection © 2008 Her Majesty Queen Elizabeth II: fig 4.5, fig 6.3, A10, C16, C17, C18, F10, F13, F42, F46

© Amgueddfa Cymru, National Museum of Wales: B38, B120

© Ashmolean Museum, Oxford: fig 3.4, A4, A5, A14

© Birmingham Museums & Art Gallery: fig 4.4, F5

© The Trustees of the British Museum: fig 2.11

© Brian Haughton Gallery, 15 Duke Street, St James's London, SW1Y 6DB: B106

© Country Life: fig 4.3

© English Heritage Photo Library: fig 1.1, C1

© Erddig, The Yorke Collection (The National Trust): A11

© The Rosalinde and Arthur Gilbert Collection, on loan to the Victoria & Albert Museum:A8

© The Worshipful Company of Goldsmiths: fig 3.7, A16, A21, A35

© Leeds Museums & Galleries: fig 3.2, fig 3.8, fig 3.10, A7, A24, B14, B20, B22, C2, C3, C4, C6, C7, C11, C21

© Museum of London: fig 5.8

© National Gallery, London: fig 1.8, F6

© The Trustees of the National Museums of Scotland: A28

© National Trust Picture Library/Andreas Von Einsiedel: fig 1.5

© National Trust Picture Library/James Mortimer: fig 4.2

© Pallant House Gallery, Chichester: fig 2.10, B52, B56, B77, B82, B83, B109, B115, B116

© Pelham Gallery, London: fig 4.6

© RIBA Library, Drawings and Archives Collections: F44

© The Royal Pavilion & Museums, Brighton & Hove: fig 2.1, fig 2.4, fig 5.1, fig 5.5, fig 5.6, fig 6.1, B25, B51, B62, D11, F21, F30, F39

© V&A Images/Victoria & Albert Museum, London: fig 1.6, fig 2.3, fig 3.6, fig 6.4, A9, A17, A26, A29, B13, C8, C27, Front page: Costume textiles & fans, D12, Front page: Books, (E6) F3

F5 Robert le Vrac de Tournières
Portrait of Richard Bateman, 1741
Birmingham Museums & Art Gallery

Photographic Credits

Boughton House, Northamptonshire: fig 4.3

The Bowes Museum, Barnard Castle, Co. Durham: C10

The Burghley House Collection: fig 3.1, fig 3.12 , A12, A30

Burton Constable Foundation: C22

Sarah Cheang: fig 6.2, fig 6.5

David Cousins: F14

The Fan Museum, London: D4, D5, D6, D7

Susanne Gronnow: A11

Gurr Johns Ltd: fig 3.11, A25

The Holburne Museum of Art, Bath: Endpapers, fig 1.2, A6, A13, C5

Martyn Gregory Gallery: fig 5.2, fig 5.4

Norfolk Museum & Archaeology Service: fig 2.8

Prudence Cuming Associates Ltd: B106

Salisbury & South Wiltshire Museum: fig 2.5

Simon Martin: fig 2.10, B52, B56, B77, B76, B82, B83, B109, B115,B116

Special Collections, Brotherton Library, University of Leeds: fig 3.5

Stephen Calloway: C30

Norman Taylor: fig 1.7, fig 3.2, fig 3.8, fig 3.10, A7, A15, A20, A24, B14, B20, B22, C2, C3, C4, C6, C7, C9, C11, C13, C14, C21, E14, F12

The Museum of Worcester Porcelain: fig 2.6, fig 2.13,fig 2.16, fig 217, B55, B60, B74, B84, B87

Wartski, London: A18, A34

A17 Teapot, Chinese, c.1680
English handle and spout, c.1750
Victoria & Albert Museum (detail)

Index